AT THE SIGN OF
THE CLENCHED FIST

AT THE SIGN OF
THE CLENCHED FIST

BY

FIONN MAC COLLA

M. MACDONALD · EDINBURGH
1967

Published by
M. Macdonald
1 & 2 Richmond Lane, Edinburgh 8

Printed by
Macdonald Printers (Edinburgh) Limited
1 & 2 Richmond Lane, Edinburgh 8

WE NEED MORE UNDERSTANDING OF HUMAN NATURE
BECAUSE THE ONLY REAL DANGER THAT EXISTS IS
MAN HIMSELF. HE IS THE GREAT DANGER, AND WE
ARE PITIFULLY UNAWARE OF IT. WE KNOW NOTHING
OF MAN, FAR TOO LITTLE. HIS PSYCHE SHOULD BE
STUDIED BECAUSE WE ARE THE ORIGIN OF ALL
COMING EVIL.

—CARL GUSTAV JUNG

Part One

I

As THIS BOOK concerns judgments I might start by pointing
out that, leaving out of account altogether the element of wilful
concealment of motive which we all indulge in from time to time
and for some of us has become a settled habit, irrespective of this
and candid as we may be with one another, our judgments on each
other still remain to some extent wrong or in some degree partial
in every case. We are faced with the impossibility of *really* comprehending another person. There will always remain too many
unknowns. All we can arrive at for the most part is a *working*
assessment of another person; if it *works* in the ordinary way of
our intercourse with him it will do, pending more complete knowledge; society can carry on on the basis of such working assessments. But really to *know* another person, to pass a complete
judgment, is beyond our powers. The picture of the world (including ourselves) that occupies his consciousness, the colour and tone
of it, are beyond our complete vision and comprehension, distorted or occluded by the content of our own consciousness; his
motives are hidden from or obscure to us—as in part they are to
himself, since they arise in large part below the level of consciousness, even it might very well be, for all we certainly know,
as far back as his pre-natal experience. Even in the case of a
husband and a wife, a parent and a child, the moment is very
likely to arrive when they look at each other and suddenly know
they are strangers to each other. [To anticipate, we are not in
any case called to pass judgment on another person, only *to be on
his side*, whereby we fulfil the whole law and the prophets.] In
short, what we *know* about another person will turn out on close
examination to be for the most part, or in varying part, not the
actual other person but our own ideas about him, not the actual
other person but the mental labels we have ourselves attached
to him. Those ideas or mental labels that we attach to another
person may truly correspond to some element in him, or they may
correspond to nothing in him and be entirely false, but the sum
of them can never in any instance add up to the totality of

another's being and actuality, with all his interacting physical and mental elements, and his motivation which may be so deeply derived as to be obscure even to himself, even misunderstood by himself.

If therefore we cannot know the brother whom we have seen, how shall we know the brethren whom we have not seen? It is astonishing how people who are perfectly willing to recognise the limitations set to their knowledge of other actual persons, their contemporaries and known to them, and accordingly to withhold the finality of their judgment in their case, have nevertheless no hesitation or sense of presumption in expressing final judgments or absolute assessments of persons necessarily unknown to them because they belonged to another country, or another culture, or another age; that is, the content of whose consciousness was different, perhaps very widely different, in colour or structure or pattern of motivation from their own or their contemporaries'. They may concede the ultimately impenetrable mystery in the personality of a neighbour or relative, yet have no sense of rashness or precipitancy in holding final views and passing absolute judgments on people in the past, in history.

The same holds of events as with persons. Every intelligent person knows by now, or ought to know, that any given number of individuals witnessing even a quite simple occurrence will give an equal number of varying accounts of it. This is so well known that if in a court of law a number of witnesses give exactly similar testimony as to a particular event, it is at once suspected that they have been together and arranged their evidence beforehand. Yet any number of people who are aware of this fact, so that they would suspect collusion if a number of persons were to give an exactly similar account of a quite simple contemporary event actually witnessed by them—a road accident, for instance—will nevertheless be found taking it for granted that they know exactly what occurred on this or that occasion in the past, even the remote past.

This curious and as we can already see totally unwarranted certainty about events and personages in the past extends to everybody, positively everybody. Even those of us who would hasten to say with a sort of rueful humility, I hated history, or, I was no good at history at school, will prove on a close scrutiny to be positively certain about a great many events in history and the character and actions of a large number of its personages. So much so that we are ready to resist any account of the events, or any view of the personages, which differs from that of which we are "certain," and to combat it with emotions ranging from bewilderment to fury, insofar as profession of such alternative views and interpretations will appear like wilful and perverse denial of manifest truth, truth which "everybody knows."

Whence is this certainty about history derived, this cetrainty which even those of us who were "no good" at history—or for that matter it may be at any subject of academic study—walk around with all our lives so that it is like something built into our consciousness of the-world-that-is-not-ourselves? Certainly not from scrutiny of the textual or other evidence, for to that we have no access short of making it a subject of specialist study, for which we are as to all but the tiniest minority both untrained and undisposed. We shouldn't know where to begin to look for the evidence. But in fact we have no sort of feeling that any such scrutiny of the sources is necessary. We are perfectly happy to leave that sort of activity to those who are equipped for it and choose to make it their occupation, *having however a perfect assurance*—and this is most curious and looks as if it ought to be significant—*that whatever facts they turn up cannot possibly contradict or cause us to have to modify those of which we are already "certain" and seem always to have been "certain."*

Let us first of all give an example or two of the sort of thing I mean—"facts" of which everyone is "certain" though unable to adduce any evidence—feeling indeed no need for evidence as the "fact" has the aspect of *self-evident* truth and always seems to have been known and known in fact to everybody. More or less at random, then: that Robert Burnes was a drunkard—("puir Rabbie!"), that Mary Queen of Scots was a wanton and murdered her husband, that the Princes in the Tower were murdered by their "wicked uncle," Richard III, that (this perhaps among the more "learned") the Emperor Tiberius was a frightful old debauchee who spent his last years in tremendous, epic orgies on the island of Capri.

The evidence for each of those "facts" rests upon nothing more solid than the testimony of the person's enemies. The first three are certainly untrue, the fourth almost certainly untrue—(it is faintly possible that Tiberius having become senile engaged—it would have had to be as a spectator, would it not?—in some sort of sensual displays, though from his known character very unlikely; the evidence is that of Tacitus, who was the enemy of his whole house—in other words an early example of a "smear" campaign by a journalist of the day).

But surely, one says, there are some categories of historical facts about which one is entitled to be certain! For instance, that there was a battle at Waterloo, in which Napoleon was defeated. That, as a statement, is certainly true. But if we carefully examine what happens in ourselves when we advert to this fact we shall soon observe that it is far more than a simple act of intellectual assent—such as takes place in our consciousness in response to the statement that two and two make four. We are sure of that too, but by way of a simple act of intellectual assent. What happens in us when we advert to the fact of Waterloo is something much more complex and more extended through the personality. If we watch ourselves very carefully—as it were "listen" to the inner event of our reactions—when we hear or see the word Waterloo, we shall observe certain muscular movements in the neighbourhood of the plexus or diaphragm, accompanied by an inflow of emotions of an uplifting and pleasant and as it were self-admiring kind; and we may recognise in this more or less the total inner event which would accompany the heart-intended shouting of the word, Hurrah! And it is this emotional uplifting and accompanying "firming-up" movements—so slight perhaps that we miss them but which would certainly be measurable by a delicate instrument—which constitutes the "meaning" of Waterloo for us. Waterloo certainly took place, as a fact to which intellectual assent may be given; but whether what Waterloo means to us, as an other than intellectual movement in the personality, ever took place is another and very different question. What *we* are "certain" of is not that there was a battle at Waterloo but that the outcome was "a good thing" and moreover in some undefined way reflected credit in advance on ourselves.

But *was* it "a good thing?" Certainly the French did not think so, and if we face the question squarely can we say on what grounds they were necessarily wrong? If we examine it with care

12

we shall find that our conviction that the outcome was a good thing is no more than *something we have always taken for granted because on every hand we have always found it taken for granted.* We have acquired our attitude regarding Waterloo not by rational conviction but absorption from our human environment, as an influence from the human climate in which we grew up, and that is no way to go about forming judgments.

(As a matter of fact writers like McNair Wilson are able to bring forward a formidable array of facts to prove that the accepted view is quite wrong, that Napoleon—two centuries before his time in comprehending the hidden financial bases of contemporary history and politics—was endeavouring to play the genuine part of the Liberator he was hailed as throughout Europe, that his desire to invade England was not an indication of an insatiable appetite for conquest but aimed purely at reaching and destroying the Money Power of International Usury centred in the City of London, which Money Power it was, for its own preservation, which continually stirred up and financed war upon *him*; and that had he succeeded the humanity of all countries—and especially of course England, and still more Scotland—would have escaped the horrors of unrestrained Capitalist Industrialism which shortly thereafter began its process of crushing them to dust. It is a formidably attested view and as such ought to appear in all textbooks of history as at the very least a *respectable alternative* view to the orthodox one, which represents the whole Napoleonic episode very simply—too, too simply—as a contest between the "good" English and their allies in league with the angels against the "bad" French misled by Napoleon and in league with the devil.)

What point have we reached now? That the consciousness of all, even the least suspecting, is furnished with solid historical "certainties"—about events in the past, about the persons involved in them, and about the propriety of the emotional and other associations evoked by them—which "certainties" are in fact by no means certain, some partially true, some demonstrably false, some materially true but illicit or at least questionably licit in their emotional, moral and other associations in consciousness.

13

Yet there can be no doubt that we derive much of our sense of security, of "knowing where we are" in our own world and our own age, from our conviction of "knowing" how things went in the past and the sort of people who were active in the process. And there can be little doubt that much, perhaps most of the extreme reluctance most of us have to revising our judgment about our favoured historical "facts," the actual resistance we put up to acceptance of alternative but better attested versions of what occurred, derives from unconscious more than conscious recognition of the threat abandonment of our cherished certainties would represent to our sense of security. Even though we were "no good at history" we "know" what history meant and means, and if we were once to be brought to abandoning one element in that structure of certainties who knows where the process might stop! We might end by having the entire structure collapse about us, leaving us in the position most of us would dread above everything, of being houseless without even a single wall of protective certainty, without even firm ground under our feet, exposed to winds and earthquakes of doubt and hesitation, compelled for dear life—a task for which most of us would consider ourselves inadequate and unequipped—to apply our minds to actual evidence and painfully and with infinite labour and much smiting of ourselves on the head and asking of ourselves the question, "Is it true?" to build up at least a shelter—(having regard to the limitations of our possible knowledge, and even of the availability of the evidence, it could scarcely ever be as solid again as our former house of certainties: on the other hand it would be roomier)— within which we could organise a less positive but more enlightened and understanding mental life, a mental life in touch with and based upon verifiable realities of the past (and also of the present, since those who lived in former times were, *mutatis mutandis* and in the broad lines of their consciousness and motivation, not such different persons from ourselves and our contemporaries, so that the more we come to know of those who went before the better placed—the more usefully placed—we shall be to understand those at present in the world), although even so we should have to get accustomed to a certain airiness in our new mental dwelling, due to the permanently unglazed condition of some of the windows, even perhaps the incompleteness of

14

some of the walls: I refer to the necessary incompleteness or sheer inaccessibility of the evidence in a great many historical contexts: the evidence is simply not there; time has covered it up: we should have to be prepared in such contexts to suspend final judgment. Are we going to submit to this—the abandonment or at the very least re-examination of all our certainties about the past, the dire passage through a prolonged period of doubt and darkness in which we should be required to engage in the excruciatingly painful and unfamiliar activity of critical assessment of evidence, in order to arrive in the end at an edifice of certainties more soundly based, it is true, but draughty and too large for comfort, having nothing like the cosy security of the building we abandoned—are we going to submit to this? The answer in most cases would be, not likely!

Our human method here would be to halt the situation somewhat before it presented itself clearly to us in consciousness, so that we could still cling with a good conscience to our certainties and allow the threat of the truth to go by.

To return to the question, whence come those certainties, which in great numbers of cases turn out not to be the truth?

In the first place let it be said that they are certainties simply because they are not the truth, or more exactly perhaps that they tend to be certainties in proportion as they are not the truth.

Truth about anything human whether of the past or present is of its nature complex, so much so that something of it will always escape even a mind proportioned or disposed to encompass it in great measure: a lie is always simpler, often so simple that it can be encompassed in a single, as it were unicellular concept, capable of being picked up in passing by quite small or inattentive minds, which makes it for most of us irresistibly attractive in that easily and without effort on our part it yields us the pleasurable and above all secure feeling of possessing knowledge. Actually all we know about a person or event may be our own simple concept or idea, the mental tag we attach to the name. This may only to a certain extent or even not at all correspond to their reality, the real truth of their being, but it has the great and for most of us the irresistible merit of conveying

15

the illusion of knowledge and therefore of security. Don't let us forget either that "knowledge means power." If Robert Burnes can be comprised within the concept "drunkard," Mary Queen of Scots within the concept "wanton," Richard III within that of "murderer" and "child-murderer" at that, the Emperor Tiberius within "senile debauchee" and so on, then anyone at all who is capable of forming the concepts "drunkard," "wanton," "child-murderer" and "senile debauchee" is able to feel not only that he "knows" but that in some fashion in his own mind he actually has power or control over Robert Burnes, Mary Queen of Scots, Richard III and the Emperor Tiberius. Very flattering indeed, even intoxicating.

And that leads us to the second reason why the lie is so much more immediately acceptable than the truth, which is that the lie, although subtly and unperceived it may be, always flatters us in our self-conceit. The concepts "drunkard," "wanton," etc., etc., which we as a matter of general practice and universal observation are extremely ready or at the very least strongly tempted to apply to others on the scantiest evidence, are always accompanied by superiority-feelings in us—psychologically speaking the superiority-feelings are the *reason* for the attachment of the concept to the name—"child-murderer," "debauchee," and a host of other appellations allow us with great facility to feel "up" with regard to even the greatest personages of the past (or present) and put them correspondingly "down" with regard to us. Our ego-feelings of self admiration or regard are constantly threatened in this life by everything—so very, very much—that is greater, more magnificent, more powerful, more brilliant than we can ever be. But if we can attach a derogatory concept to another person whether in the present or the past, we are able to feel we have disposed of their giftedness, power, brilliance or magnificence, pushed it away from contact with us, and so protected our ego and liberated it just as it is. Those two facts, that it is always simpler, usually very simple, in structure and therefore demands no effort from us before yielding the satisfaction- and security-feelings that go with knowledge, and secondly that it invariably gives free scope to our ego-feelings of power, superiority and self-regard, explain why, as someone has said, "a lie will girdle the earth while truth is putting on his boots."

The familiar Latin tag has it, *Magna est veritas et praevalebit*, Truth is great and it will prevail. Anything more untrue could hardly be stated: truth seldom if ever—and for the reasons given —overtakes the lie. So far as history is concerned such an overtaking would require first of all that the truth be discovered and presented, which would require on somebody's part a most unusual combination of qualities, not to say opportunities—access to the facts, an attitude of true inward docility in their presence, an ability to detect and identify in himself prior occluding attitudes and emotional conditioning and to allow for them, forensic skill in presentation—and, one might add, very importantly, a publisher willing to risk publishing unpopular and unheard-of views. On the other part it would require an individual here and there happening to encounter this favoured person's published work and prepared for it on his own account by similar unusual qualities of a critical faculty and a similar inward attitude of true docility, combined with a most unusual introspective gift whereby he might be able to detect, track down and neutralise his own prior conditioning over the field in question—and, one might add, a sort of mental tight-rope-walker's ability to tread the often thin strand of the definitely ascertained stretched across the abyss of the what must remain forever unknown because time has been at work to erode the evidence. No, once the lie has got going, especially once it has received official sanction, truth is exceedingly unlikely ever to overtake it.

Once again to the question, Whence do we derive those certainties—I am speaking now more specifically about history—of which even those of us who make the least pretensions to any sort of knowledge prove on examination to have a surprising number, which we carry about with us like a sort of structure of "known fact" which represents for us the surroundings of our personal, conscious life and within which we live as behind a protective shield of the "self-evidently-true," so that we "don't need to worry" about uncertainties?

The first that springs to mind will doubtless be the school, where most of us receive practically all of our formal instruction as to what we are to believe about what happened before we were in the world—and of course in a great many other things as well, not necessarily unrelated to history, as for instance taste, what we are to admire in literature, and so on. But the matter doesn't end there—in school—and in fact it didn't even begin there. From our earliest conscious moments we are subject to influences which come to us from those about us, whoever they may be, which begin to cause the formation of rudimentary ideas and a pattern of emotions associated with them, and this not so much by anything *said to* us as by words and statements *overheard* by us, and above all by the tones of the voices in which the statements are made or the words pronounced in our hearing—(I come of a race of soldiers, right in the mainstream of the Scottish cannon-fodder tradition, and I still recollect, from the conversations that went on above me in infancy, the resonant and deeply self-congratulatory tone that mingled with the delivery of, for instance, the name, Waterloo). So that we come to school with a number of ideas part-formed already about the past and some of the events and persons in it, and a certain set of emotions all ready to be triggered off in us by mention of certain names of events or persons which we have heard spoken of in tones unintendedly pregnant with judgments of one kind or another.

And those rudimentary ideas and early emotional reactions to certain words and names are certainly not of a kind to be altered or lessened by any formal instruction we subsequently receive in school; on the contrary the ideas will only become sharpened and better defined and the emotional reactions and associations stronger and more immediate, since after all the persons by whom we were originally influenced had been speaking out of the formations in consciousness they had themselves received in school in their day, having been similarly prepared in their own pre-school stage by statements and tones of voice overheard and emotional reactions absorbed from their own elders, who had in turn in their day been formed in their judgment and pattern of emotional associations in school, and so on. Furthermore no influence we are likely to encounter in our out-of-school days or our after-school lives will ever be of a kind to counteract the system of ideas and associated emotions in which we have been instructed and with which we have been charged in that part of our school training that had to do with the formation of our ideas about and our feelings about the past. For identical judgments and an identical value system where the past is concerned will in fact be implied even when not explicitly stated in everything we are likely to see or hear for the rest of our lives, in the conversations we take part in or overhear, in the newspapers and books we read, and, if we have a religious connection, from the pulpits we sit under. What it amounts to is this, that there is a general view or judgment of the past, and a particular view or judgment of numbers of actors in it, which is so universal in our society that it comes to us practically with the air we breathe, so that consciously or—still more, and more potently when—unconsciously it conditions all our thinking and judgments upon human affairs, and simply because it has been imbibed or inhaled with the air during our whole life even more than formally imposed in our impressionable years, appears to us so self-evidently true that any questioning of its validity is bound to have the look of wilful perversity if not of partaking in some degree of lunacy.

What is this view of the past which is assumed on all sides to have an absolute validity, to be the obvious and self-evident truth about history, and how did it come to be formed and then imposed?

To take the second question first; the first thing to realise is that it is *a* view and that it *was* formed, that is, that it was constructed in certain minds at a certain time. The point to grasp here is that in any struggle victory confers upon the winning side the right to write the history that will be believed by the succeeding generations. To take examples far enough away from us for our own conditioned pattern of emotion-judgments not to be called into play, had Hitler won the last war the "history" now being taught in German schools and propagated in countless books and newspapers and permeating and diffused by countless conversations would be vastly different from what is in fact being taught and propagated and beginning to be "breathed-in" by the present generation of Germans whether of East or West. Had the Communist revolution failed in Russia and victory gone to the Kerensky democrats, the history now being taught in Russian schools and taken for granted as the "obvious" truth about history by the whole present generation of Russians would have been vastly different from the view now actually held and assumed to be the only possible and "obvious" view. Whereas had the Revolution failed altogether—which it might well have done: it was touch and go—the "self-evidently true" view of history taken by "all intelligent Russians" and permeating the intellectual and emotional atmosphere of the whole country today, would have been something totally different again; Marxism, for instance, far from having any importance would be known only to students of philosophy as a curious German-Jewish mental aberration and to students of history as associated with an ill-conceived attempt made at one time to overthrow the lawful and established order, an attempt which all would agree fortunately failed; its success would be something unthinkable. Again, had the French Revolution failed it is easy to realise that the consciousness of the French people today and for the last now nearly two centuries would have been of a vastly different sort and complexion from what it in fact is, in that the Revolution—insofar as it was a part of it at all—would have figured in it as a fortunately unsuccessful aberration, an attempt against the true and rational order of things made by a handful of fanatic men under the influence of—or under the cloak of—a set of crazy, romantic notions. The *only* reason why this is not the view of "all intelligent Frenchmen" today and for the last two centuries is that in fact the Revolution did succeed, and as a consequence its supporters gained the power to dictate what was to be written as history and believed by all subsequent generations, so that it came to be an inescapable element in the very atmosphere of France, breathed in by the great majority of Frenchmen all their lives and consequently assumed to be "self-evidently true," not to be denied by anyone who coveted a reputation for good sense and good faith.

It has been no whit different in our own case; we also have had a "view" of history imposed upon us, permeating the air about us—or can we suppose that of all the systems of historical "certainty" current (because imposed) in all the areas of the earth, ours alone by some extraordinary chance corresponds to *true* history? Truth in the mind consists in conformity with its object;

in the case of history this would require an almost infinite conformity since the object in this case is almost infinite—nothing less in the end than everything that has been thought, done or felt by men. The greatest minds might apply themselves to it for a lifetime, or rather to that portion of it of which evidence remains, and scarcely escape the error of prematurity of systematisation, the imposition of a subjective pattern on the material—there have been some lamentable instances among great historical "names" in recent decades. Bearing this in mind, along with the other fact already agreed to, that we can arrive at only a partial judgment or understanding even of other actual persons, our contemporaries and known to us, we can hardly fail to begin to perceive that our own structure of historical "certainties" can be nothing more than —as Bernard Shaw defined "history"—"a falsehood agreed upon," a structure of historical certainties devised with a view to their own self-justification and self-perpetuation by some party or "side" which at some point or other were the "winning side," and imposed on succeeding generations by "teachers" or opinion-formers of all kinds, whether in schools or outside them, who themselves knew nothing of history except for what they themselves had acquired from textbooks of the official "view" or breathed in from the air of their age.

Now that we know how our system of historical certainties came to be imposed—that it *has been imposed,* and before that was *com*posed, and by a "winning side," let us return to the question: What is this view of the past which is assumed on all sides to have an absolute validity, to be the obvious and self-evident truth about history?

If we look closely within ourselves, so as to catch a glimpse of the characteristic movement of our will and emotions and ideas working together in the act of thinking about history, we shall see that we have already although perhaps without realising it come very close to identifying a major and general principle of all such thinking. It consists in this, that *we take it for granted that in history the winning side was always right.*

A contemporary philosopher (Professor Ayer) has recently castigated "the argument, to which Marxists are especially prone, that we have a duty to support the winning side" on the ground that —obviously, one should have thought—it "illicitly extracts a value judgment from what is supposed to be a neutral statement of fact." It may be that Marxists are especially prone to this as an argument: it is certain that we are all given to it, and all the time, as an unformulated and for the most part unconscious assumption. It is the major and most characteristic mark of all our historical thinking.

Let us only look back over our "knowledge" of history and we shall see that it is so. Take for instance a sufficiently far away and "neutral" event—the ancient Romans. Have we not always taken it for granted as "obvious" that the advance of Rome to imperial greatness was in the natural course of things—"a good thing," meriting and requiring our approval as it went on step by step? Of course we have, and even to the extent of identifying ourselves with them in their career. Even those of us who were "no good at history" have always understood perfectly that the growth of Rome was something it was absolutely necessary to approve of—even though we might have heartily wished in school that the Romans would get on with the business and not pile up so many "facts" and dates for us to learn. We might even on this score feel a distinct impatience with if not a hearty disapproval of the various peoples who, as we felt, out of perverseness kept on opposing the Romans and holding up the process. But that it was necessary and right that the Romans should win, of this we never had any doubt; it was in the nature of things—it was "history."

But this, as we can now see, was "an illicit value judgment." Was it "a good thing" that the Romans won? According to the Romans of course, yes. But according to the Greeks? according to the Etruscans? according to the Gauls? according to the Carthaginians? Who says those peoples' preference for their own way of life over the Romans' was invalid? The Romans were not only a very cruel, they were in some ways a very limited people; they were not only heavy-handed, they were also heavy-footed. There is no reason whatsoever to doubt that Greeks and Gauls, Etruscans and Carthaginians, save for the Romans, would have produced in their own cultures many facets

22

of brilliance not included in the whole range of Roman potentiality; and to this extent humanity must have been many times the loser by the Romans' success. We have no reason for assuming, as we always have, that Roman civilisation was identical with *civilisation itself*, because no absolute standards exist which can be applied to human societies and their ways of life—and even if they did we should be unable to apply them since we are in fact involved in the way of life of our own particular society and unable to stand outside it to make our judgment. Of the Roman Empire we cannot validly say, This happened, therefore it was "a good thing": we cannot licitly go beyond the statement, This happened.

And now look what happens to us with our principle that it is of moral obligation to support the winning side. It comes to the fifth century, and the Roman Empire is invaded and destroyed by wave after wave of Teutonic barbarians. This also, according to our principle, we are bound to regard, and do regard, and were taught in school to regard as "a good thing." First we accept and approve the advance of Rome because the Romans were "civilised" and their conquests were "necessary and inevitable," and a little later we are on the same principle accepting and approving the advance of the Teutonic barbarians because they were "uncivilised" and it was the destruction of the Roman Empire that was now "necessary and inevitable." This contradiction we are quite happy to accept as some sort of law of history; what was "a good thing" at one time became "a bad thing" somewhat later; the winning side was always right; "history" demanded that whatever happened should have happened.

Actually there is no such thing as such a "law of history"—as a matter of fact there is no such thing as *any* "law of history": if there were *we* should never be able to perceive it, because we should require to stand outside the historical process in order to do so. The most we can licitly dare to say is that the Romans won because they won, and when the barbarian invasions came some centuries later that they lost because they lost. The reasons for their winning or losing were bound up with all sorts of human considerations—material, moral or concerning "morale,'" economic—but they had nothing to do with any "law of history." What we do know and should keep better in mind is that both processes involved enormous and unimaginable human suffering and the extinction of we can never know what potentiality of alternative human achievement.

Fortunately the wailing, screaming and crying of the enormous numbers of actual human beings whose butchery or enslavement accompanied both those movements of conquest could not penetrate to and were inaudible from the studies of "historians" and writers of "history" where they sat happily and with a sense of power—*power*, that is the thing!—constructing "historical laws" and systems of historical "interpretation" which existed nowhere except where they were being created, inside their own heads—until, that is, through the influence of their works, which in many cases became or were actually written as textbooks—"classics" of "history" in fact—they came to exist inside our heads also and those of all our contemporaries, and our predecessors for as far back as they were subject to the mind-forming influences of educational media such as schools and churches, universities, books, magazines and newspapers.

The view that we have a duty to support the winning side in history, then, is not justifiable in the light of the facts of history, and results from the illicit importation of value judgments into what ought to be no more than neutral statements. It still remains to enquire why this particular view of history should, first, have been so readily and frequently fallen upon by "historians" and, second, have proved down the generations so readily acceptable and easily assimilable by their public.

There is unquestionably a danger at the present time in the tendency in various contexts to "turn everything into psychology." All the same the mind has its characteristic ways of working in the process of dealing with the data of external reality in the attempt to turn it into the content of consciousness or in other words possess it in the form of knowledge. In the process it is likely to impose something of itself on the external data. So much so that in general what we hold in the form of internal truth, truth in the mind, equals external reality plus another element contributed by the mind in the act or process of "knowing" it. In proportion as the element contributed by the mind or prior content of consciousness preponderates in the act of knowledge over the element of external reality, we have error. If we want to arrive at possession of the real truth of outer things, therefore, we require to be on our guard against a too active participation of subjective elements in the process.

The common way in which the mind proceeds in the acquisition of knowledge is by the use of categories, that is to say the mind approaches external reality provided as it were with a number of containers or receptacles labelled as regards their contents, into which it proceeds to fit the new external reality encountered—let us hope without too much distortion of the external reality in the process of fitting it in. We are not provided with those categories or "containers" ready-made, of course, like so many boxes furnishing the mind, so many to each person, to some more, to some fewer: we construct them as we go along, to accommodate the content of experience: the danger lying in our failing to see that a particular item of new experience requires the manufacture of a new category or sub-category to fit it, or even (for the moral question enters into or at any rate touches the process of knowledge-construction as it touches everything) in our simply being averse from the effort, preferring the easy, undemanding course of crushing the newly encountered reality into an already existing category, indifferent to any damage done to it or to the error of its now being wrongly labelled. The larger the mind, the more apt for knowledge and the more it is in possession of real knowledge, the larger will be the number of its categories in use and the greater the number of their internal divisions or sub-containers—and of course the more constant the willingness to make where necessary the effort to construct new categories. While of course the really large mind as we have already seen will always have considerable areas between the categories or containers representing if only for the time being suspensions of judgment, labelled, if labelled at all, "possibilities and probabilities," "classifications-pending."

The simplest and most primitive way in which to approach any area of external reality is to do it provided with only two categories, the one for external realities that evoke a sympathetic response in us such as might be represented by a positive, Yes, this category labelled simply, "Good," and the other for those external realities which evoke an unsympathetic or hostile response in us corresponding to the negation, No, and labelled simply, "Bad." (I was to have said labelled White and Black, but we live in a world in which white is coming to be regarded as black, and black as white; there would have been a danger of some confusion, so plain "good" and "bad" will have to serve). What historians of the winning-side-is-always-right school have done, then, is to approach the material of history armed with this most primitive of mental mechanisms. The enormous complexities of actual history have by the dualising activity of historians' minds been reduced to non-existence, and all that remains are two stark categories, the "bad" and the "good," those to whom we say, hurrah! and those to whom we say, not likely! or words to that effect. Every conflict in history is a plain contest between a bad side and a good side, with the good side invariably emerging the victor because that is the nature of things; that is "history."

Now where have we met all this before? Of course! in children's stories, or stories of the American West. In those also the protagonists are not persons (persons are complex, persons change with experience, and certainly are never simply good or bad)—but "characters" or types, who are changeless and clearly divided into "good men" and "bad men." It is the universal characteristic of such tales that after an exciting struggle the "good men" triumph and the "bad men" get their deserts. That is as it should be, for such is the nature of the tale. It is another matter that historians, whose concern is exclusively with persons —not "characters" or abstractions who live with the life of the author's mind, but persons, who lived with their own life— —should have fobbed us off for all those generations with an account of a "history" which is nothing more in essence than an enormously extended contest of "baddies" and "goodies" garnished with a more or less learned paraphernalia of facts and dates and names and places.

There is of course a subjective reason of the kind that lurks below consciousness, for the very ready acceptance of this sort of interpretation of history, and it is that the simple dualising approach, with only two rigid categories into which everything has perforce to be divided, liberates us at a stroke from all the complexities, not to say perplexities, all the nuances, all the difficulties of access to evidence, all the doubts and doubtfulnesses and necessary suspensions of judgment of actual history "out there," and confers on us the satisfying sensations of knowledge at the cost of no more effort than is required to distinguish between yes and no. *To dualise your material is the quickest and easiest way to feel you possess it and have power over it.* It is also, where any question of humanity is involved, the surest way to falsify it.

But this winning-side-is-always-right interpretation of history has a further and still more serious implication. If the earliest set of "goodies" eventually become "baddies" who are overcome by a fresh set of "goodies" who in turn after a time become "baddies" and are overcome by a new lot of "goodies" and so on and on till we come to our own day, it is manifest and necessary that each set of "goodies" must be "better" than the set of "goodies" who preceded them. It follows of necessity that *we*, representing the latest set of "goodies," are the "best" of the whole lot. The theory that the winning side is always right, translated into plain terms, says simply: History proves that I and my contemporaries are in every way better than any men who existed in the past, and the better the farther back in time you go. Not often, it is true, will a historian go so far as to state this in precisely those terms or their equivalents, but then he has no need to, the winning-side-is-always-right theory says it perfectly clearly by implication, and the implication is enough for that subjective element—a sort of reason too—which, in addition to and simultaneously with the rational, conscious reason, works in us on the same data of experience but at a level below the rationally conscious. What this sub-rational, sub-conscious element is concerned with in any confrontation with external reality, is not the degree of objective rational truth that can be perceived in it, but the degree to which it liberates or constrains the ego. When we say that a statement—in history, for instance, although it might be in any other context—is true, we *may* mean that we have reached a conviction of truth in its regard as the end act of a process of reasoning: but what, unless

27

we are very watchful, we are equally likely to mean is that the statement has been the occasion for a feeling of liberation in us arising from deep down below the conscious—in which case the "proof" of the statement's truth has not been the perception of its rational validity but a sense of liberation which it occasioned. A statement causes us to feel liberated; we don't stop to look within and see exactly what has been liberated—in any case most of us have no skill or practice in introspection—so we take it that our feeling of liberation means the statement is true. Conversely if a statement occasions an apprehension of something to be constrained in us we take this to be an indication of its falsity and our inner movement in repudiation of it as the rejection of error. Most of us "reason" in this way much of the time in our daily lives in every context: many of us hardly know any other way to "reason." Yet it is quite a different thing from real or rational reason, which is a movement of the *intellect* in an objective context or with an objective reference; whereas this way of "reason," this manner of recognition of "truth" and "error," concerns a movement of the *will* in a subjective context, which the objective statement only evokes or stimulates or occasions within the area of our subconscious.

That the winning side was always right is not a fact—but it looks like the truth. It looks like the truth because such a view, carrying the unmistakable implication that contemporary man is essentially "better" than all who went before, and the more the further back you go, is so tremendously flattering, and liberates such a flood of superiority-feelings in us, that we seem at once to recognise its truth, not suspecting that the faculty which has recognised this "truth" is the will, which is not the faculty by which we are able to apprehend truth, and not the intellect, which is. That is what makes this sort of conviction so immovable: it is not susceptible of rational disproof because it was not in the first place perceived by the intellect but on the contrary acclaimed by the will, to the accompaniment of thunderous applause from all the emotions of a self-approving type. Every time thereafter that this "truth" occurs to mind there is an inward burst of self-regard and its truth is recognised all over again, so much so that we are puzzled, saddened, annoyed, or even infuriated by anyone who would deny—citing *rational* reasons—so self-evident a "truth." So much so that even if we possess an active intellectual faculty and by means of it come to perceive the validity of the rational disproof of one of those "self-evident truths," we shall continue in spite of ourselves—at any rate for a long time and probably to some extent to the end of our days—to experience the same affirming movement of the will and the same pleasurable, self-approving emotions whenever the said though now disproved "truth" is encountered; simply because the association of the "truth" with that movement of the emotions was originally formed below the rational level and its tendency will be, for reasons of its own preservation, to resist opposition or contradiction from the upper plane of the rational and fully conscious. *The subconscious has its reasons, and they tend to be more potent and more resistant than the reasons that are formed in full and rational consciousness.*

If our aim were to conduct the formation of our views and judgments whether of private persons and situations or on large and public issues and matters of past or contemporary history purely on the plane of the rational and fully conscious—as heaven knows there is the most urgent need that it should be—we should have to remain continuously on the look out for the invasion of prior views consolidated with their accompanying emotions in the region of the personality below the rational and fully conscious, so as to identify them and endeavour by a deliberate conscious act to set them aside or at least make continuous allowance for the influence of their presence. It will be exhausting work, for it will involve something like looking with great vigilance in two directions at once, as it were keeping an eye on the outer object and on ourselves simultaneously, and the temptation will be to weary of the effort and relapse upon old attitudes, which may not correspond with reality but at least solace us with the comfort and security of old, familiar, self-admiring emotions: we may not be right about history but at least we will be again on good terms with ourselves!

But the doctrine that the winning side is always right (and it is our duty to support it) is open to an objection of the gravest kind from yet another direction. If we look at it carefully we shall begin to perceive something very peculiar indeed—nothing less than that it implies the presence all through history of an element which does not belong to history. Why is it our duty always to support the winning side? Because the winning side is always *right*—not, note, stronger: to that we should agree, if in "stronger" is implied every fact or accident which at any point may give one side the victory over another—not stronger, but *right*, so that it is our *moral* duty to support the side that wins.

Take at will or at random any juncture in history where a contest is to be decided. There are the two contestants, joined in the conflict. To the ordinary eye, the eye of a contemporary for instance, they would seem to fill the field. But not to the eye of the historian of the winning-side-is-always-right school, which includes most historians of one kind or another, especially those who write textbooks for the young. To this sort of historian the field must leave room for a third party, albeit invisible, *namely the element whose part it is to ensure that the "right" side wins*. Were it not so who knows but at some time or other the "wrong" side might win, whereupon history would of necessity collapse and lose its meaning. There is no getting away from it, if we say the winning side has always been right throughout history, we are implying in history the presence of some constant element, invisible, immaterial, supernatural, magical, however you conceive it, which was unknown to the contesting parties, the actors in the drama, but was nevertheless more potent and important than they, since its role was to guide events and ensure that the "right" thing happened.

There was in fact no such force in history, perpetually and irresistibly pushing events in the right direction. The idea is a pure superstition. We not infrequently find ourselves or overhear others talking, with much implied superiority, of what we designate the superstitions of men of other ages, or other cultures in the present. The men of every age have their superstitions, not recognised by them as such. There can be little doubt that to a person standing outside our Western age and culture this superstition of ours—the belief in what we may call the Third Party Necessarily Present in history—would appear as absurd as any that ever conditioned and distorted human understanding.

For it is, of course, this we-must-approve-the-winning-side doctrine, merely one way of expressing what has been called "the most fatuous of all historical fallacies," the great myth of "Progress." Fatuous and a fallacy it certainly is: nonetheless in one form or another, whether in the side to side and up and up movement favoured by Hegelians and Marxists or the unilinear, straightforward advance which is the common conception among us—everything simply getting better and better and better down the centuries—in whatever form it is conceived the myth of Progress has dominated the mind of the West for many generations, as someone has said, "with the force of a religion." In part no doubt it represented the transference of the concept of biological evolution into the social order, and of course it has appeared to be justified to many by the huge advances in science, industry and technology of recent and adjacent times.

However it grew up—the question is too large to detain us here—a fallacy the notion of Progress is, and of the most fatuous sort, inhabiting the mind of Western man in defiance of all the evidence and representing the intrusion into the field of an illicit element contributed by the mind itself, and whose origins are in philosophy or mythology and not in history. It is much more than an idea—if it were only that it could be held as it were apart from the mind, bombarded by the evidence, broken up and dissipated—it has come to be a part of the *way in which* Western man thinks. It is not so much an item in the content of the mind as a mode or manner of the mind's operation. As such it is of course unconscious and all but ineradicable. For myself I must admit that I read history and (heaven forgive me) taught and wrote about it for twenty years before I gradually became conscious that meshed in with all my thinking about history was a cog of a different metal, something which might have been among things of its own kind in philosophy or mythology perhaps, but certainly had no business in anything connected with history. And although a further thirty years have passed since then I have even yet to be unceasingly vigilant lest I discover myself again thinking about some element in the human story *as if* it were part of a well known tale which began far down among the roots of the primitive and rose and rose by successive stages, each one "better" than the last, until inevitably and of necessity it reached the in every way

31

superior "betterness" of our own time. To anyone who knows what history really says, its complex and profoundly fluctuating course, it must as a world view seem pathetic and naive. Nevertheless it is a view that we all of us take for granted in the West, so much so that it plays an unsuspected, undiscerned part in all our judgments about history—so much so that even when, as very seldom happens, we have become aware of its presence and are on our guard against its influence it still contrives to inhere tenaciously in the substance of our judgments. We cannot be surprised at this: Progress as a myth pervades the atmosphere we breathe from our first conscious moments, reaching a fury of instigation during our years in school, from which a "successful" pupil, one in whose case education has "taken," goes forth characterised more than anything else by an exalted and keenly thankful sense of the superiority of his own age and culture and generation. Thenceforward he will be able to look squarely at historical evidence in flat disproof of Progress, and even consciously accept the evidence insofar as the particular case in history is concerned, without the influence of the myth being in the least contracted in his mind, simply because "Progress" is far more than an opinion held, it has become for us in the West a characteristic of our way of thinking, a part of our conception of life itself.

We can encounter illustrations of this any day by listening-in carefully to the sort of conversations that go on around us. We may, for instance, overhear someone taking the most pessimistic view of the prospects of humanity, even to prognosticating for all mankind an imminent and violent end. Yet if we listen further we shall almost invariably discern that the same individual views, as something self-evidently true, the whole history of humanity up till now as having produced itself under the rule of a "law" of "Progress," everything moving of necessity ever forward, ever upward. If you contest his pessimistic prognostications he will rebut your argument: if you refute his "law" of "Progress" he will rebut you equally, remaining happily unaware that in logic the one excludes the other. Thus, if Progress is a law inherent in the movement of history itself, then it is not open to any individual or group whatsoever to halt, divert or bring the course of history to an end—because, that is, as part of history they are themselves subject to a law which governs all history: on the other hand, if it is within the power of any individual or group whatsoever on their own initiative or for any reason of their own to halt, divert, or bring the course of history to an end, then there can be no law of Progress—or for that matter any other law—to which history as a whole is subject.

Nor is there in fact any such law. "Progress" is merely one, or a variant of one, of those "Philosophies of History" of which there have been a great number, all false. There can be no such thing as a true Philosophy of History. If it is philosophy it is not history, and if it is history it is not philosophy. To be a philosopher of history means claiming that history follows a pattern or design which is unknown to the men who act out the events of history, but which they are nevertheless, all unknown to themselves, compelled without possibility of evasion to carry out, which pattern or design has a meaning in itself, which is in fact the Meaning of History, but which is different from the meaning of the events as it was understood by those who brought them about or suffered from them; and finally that you, the philosopher of history, understand that Meaning because you perceive that grand Pattern or Design—even though neither you nor anybody else has any idea how much of it has as yet been woven, or alternatively how much of it has yet to be woven, so that you are arguing from a fragment whose proportions in relation to the whole must remain unknown to you, an occupation which having regard to the incalculably enormous possibilities, in thought and action both, of that unimaginable but certain to be surprising creature, man-yet-unborn, would seem to be decidedly more hazardous than that of the hopeful palaeontologist who would set out to reconstruct the anatomy of a monster extinct animal from a half-inch fragment of bone.

The fact is that *every* "philosophy of history," whether those that see in history a continuous unilinear "progress," ever on and on and up and up, or those that discern a wavy, up and down advance, or those that perceive a dialectical or side to side and upward movement, or those that see history as a series of contiguous completed circles or as reproducing again and again the life-story of plants—every Philosophy of History is a version of what we may call the Myth or Fallacy of the *Third Party Necessarily Present*—a sort of Undistributed Muddle. That is to say, no matter with what learning they may be set forth—and some have come from the historian-philosopher's study accompanied by a positively superhuman mountain of "facts"—they all agree in one thing, that they imagine or presuppose or claim to see in any historical moment more than the human occupants varyingly employed, something in the form of a third Party—Mind, or Force, or Will, whatever they choose to call it—acting *directly* on the situation, irrespective of the objectives, fully or otherwise comprehended, of the humanity of the place and time. There has been no such Third Force or Party active in history, the Design or Pattern in history is contributed by the historian-philosopher's imagination, and the Arch-Mind or Master-Will supposed to have moulded or shaped the course of events has in fact a quite different function, that of being the supreme or supernatural Guarantor of the philosopher-historian's notions.

Some of the consequences of those Design-in-history theories are hilarious. As all of them are agreed that whatever actually happened in history happened because it had to happen, because it was the right thing, this leaves Divine Providence, Hegelian National Idealism, Dialectical Materialism and a dozen other Philosophies of History in hearty and full agreement with one another. What a spectacle—the Holy Ghost arm in arm with Karl Marx both giving history a hearty shove in the same direction, towards a series of events equally desired by both. Historical superstition makes odd comrades.

It is not intended to argue, of course, that Divine Providence plays no part in history. What is superstitious is the belief—commonly, and wrongly, supposed to be Christian—that it acts in the way stated, that is as a Third Party or Force acting directly upon events irrespective of the human persons involved and their aims and objectives conscious and unconscious. Indeed such a notion precludes the very idea of Providence. Providence can only act, obviously, by preserving a creature in being according to the law of its proper nature. And the proper nature of man is among other things to possess free will. So that while it is to be hoped that he will make the fullest and most constant use of all the aids offered him by Divine Providence, his history must remain his to make or mar: otherwise his freedom of choice is an illusion and he is a blind puppet moved by he knows not what. (It may be useful to point out that somewhere in this area lies in large part the answer to the question so often heard as to why if Providence exists there is so much evil in the world: men cannot think badly and act wrongly and then call upon Providence to get them out of the morass of troubles they have got themselves into.)

Similarly, no one could deny that Dialectical Materialism has made a considerable impact on history in the last half-century. But it has done so only through the actions of men animated and energised by it as a belief. On its own account Dialectical Materialism is unable to impinge on anything, because it does not exist—outside minds. To think of it as "out there" from the beginning in history pushing events this way and that all unknown to the participators and towards ends they never conceived, is but another form of the Superstition of the Third Party Necessarily Present in history. (Nor do Marxists escape this dilemma by professing to repudiate a "mechanistic" interpretation of Dialectical Materialism: if history is conceived of under no matter what form as *bound* to follow a certain course, as Marxists view it, there you have a form of the Fallacy of the Third Party Necessarily Present, and from that there is no escape).

And so it is with every Philosophy or Design-system of history. The most we can ever say of any society is that *if* it acts in such-and-such a way, such-and-such results are likely to follow. We may risk saying, for instance, that *if* humanity starts throwing H-bombs at each other civilisation as we know it is scarcely likely to survive—or, as someone has put it, the war next following will be fought with stone clubs. *But it is always open to any society under the influence of a new idea or set of ideas*—a new religion, for instance—*to change its way of life and set off on a new course*: it has happened again and again in history and it can never be predicted.

The myth of Progress is a remarkable example—though far from the only one in our society—of the ability of an idea—or emotion-idea, for it is welded of both elements—once it has taken

35

hold upon the mind, to withstand and to survive the assault of no matter how many or how cogent facts that plainly disprove it. History shows as numerous examples of decline and retrogression among societies as of advance and progress. Let us take but one: —but one example is sufficient in itself of course to dispose of the notion that change in history must inevitably be in the direction of progress—Following the fall of the Western Roman Empire in the fifth century under the successive waves of invading Germanic tribes—Goths, Franks, etc.—the Eastern Roman or Byzantine Empire, with its capital at Constantinople, continued, and for no less than one thousand years, to be one of the best governed and culturally most brilliant areas that ever were on the surface of the earth. When it eventually fell, in the mid-fifteenth century, it fell to the Osmanli or Ottoman Turks. And the Turks were among the most savage as they were the most non-cultural or anti-cultural people who ever founded an empire. They were not only themselves non-culture-bearing, they were completely resistant to culture whenever they encountered it.

There is an observable tendency in societies that become Muhammedan to follow a certain course. First there is a wave of violent and destructive expansion, an explosion into new territories; when that wave subsides there may be a period of intellectual and artistically brilliant activity touched off by contact with the cultures submerged by the first wave or with which the Muhammedans in their new territories find themselves in contact —as for instance the Moorish civilisation in Spain which reached a point of great brilliance in philosophy and architecture and the decorative arts: the Arabs in their first destructive wave may have used the priceless volumes of the great library of Alexandria to heat the water for their baths, but later they took over Greek philosophy, carried it on, and even taught it to the Latin West— and Algebra, of course is an Arabic name: then follows the third stage, when Muhammedanism becomes completely static and inert, like a petrified ocean; and this stage—so far as has yet been seen—continues indefinitely.

The Turks contrived to miss the second stage altogether. Their history shows only the violent, expanding wave, followed directly by the petrified sea. Wherever they went they could do nothing but destroy. Culturally they brought nothing with them, and they were incapable of absorbing anything culturally from the peoples they conquered or came in contact with. Of all the peoples that have made a mark in history they must have been culturally and intellectually the most completely and utterly null. Yet they followed and replaced the thousand year long brilliance of Byzantium. It was not only not a "progress," it was a lapse or retrogression of the most absolute kind and represented an absolute loss to the human community.

Nor was there anything in the least "necessary" or "inevitable" about it. The Eastern Empire of Byzantium fell simply because it proved impossible on its own resources to sustain year after year, century after century, the incessant attacks from all directions and at various times of Arabs, Turks, Slavs, Bulgars— to say nothing of the hostility and treachery of the "Latin" or Catholic West—in fact superficially Christianised Germanic barbarians: as for instance in the so-called Fourth Crusade of 1204 when the "Latins" sacked Constantinople and attempted to set up, and did set up for a time, an Empire of their own in its territories, a blow from which the Byzantine Empire never recovered. The fall of the Byzantine Empire and the succession of the Turkish Empire therefore was not inevitable, neither was it necessary, and so far from marking a movement of Progress it marked precisely the contrary, the replacement of the highest and brightest in culture and social life by the lowest and dullest, and for all time.

This is only one example of dozens that could be cited in which Progress in history worked markedly in reverse.

If there are at least as many examples of decline and decay of societies in history as of progress, and anyone with a partially opened eye can read this in history for himself, what can be the reason for the persistence of the idea of Progress and its domination of the mind especially of the nineteenth century and into our own time? We have already seen that it represents the illicit application of biological conceptions to the lives of societies, and that the enormous expansion of industry and invention during the period lent it an appearance of striking if superficial plausibility. It is also a fact that the writers of history prior to the first decades of the present century were working over a limited field. For them history practically began with Greece and Rome, whereas since their time numbers of entire civilisations from the more distant past and more distant parts of the earth have swung up into our view. (There is also the fact of lamentable potency that great numbers read no history at all, but are satisfied with the sort of half-formed notions they find in vogue round about them.)

All the same, such immovable persistence of an idea in the face of so much proof to the contrary seems in need of deeper explanation. In such a case, where proof laid before the intellect appears to have no acceptance, one is always safe to suspect that the will may be at work, usurping the place of the intellect as the faculty whereby truth is "perceived." Is there any reason why the will should evince such readiness to "perceive" truth in the idea of Progress?

The best way to answer that is to ask, what are the effects in us of the acceptance or "perception" of such a "truth" as "Progress?" The answer is clear, it is the liberation in us, the latest dwellers on the earth, of feelings of limitless superiority. Think of it: I may be the commonplace person I see every time I look in the glass, my job boring and repetitive, my companions small-minded and poor-spirited, and so on; my whole life in a word uncreative and unheroic, compound of mediocrity and insignificance. (No need to labour this: a whole literature has grown up, on both sides of the Atlantic, on the theme of the essential pettiness and senselessness of the life of modern, civilised man; only his frantic plungings into distractions and "escape" and the liveliness of his biological urges at least throughout the earlier part of his life, hide the fact from him.) But given the assurance that history subscribes to an ineluctable law of Progress, I and my contemporaries must of necessity and in spite of everything form a society "better" in every way than anything that ever existed before, and are in an absolute way entitled to look down on even the greatest figures of the past—one recalls such of their names as one has heard with feelings of condescending patronage, and they appear before the imagination as rather quaint and absurd puppet-creatures worked up about nothing, creatures who "hadn't a clue" and were in fact something less than three-dimensional: we have the feeling life wasn't quite *real* in their days. This sense of essen-

38

tial superiority over immense numbers of men of the past we carry about with us, and every time we consciously advert to it we feel exalted: it is our compensation for mediocrity and our never-ending consolation. . . . We shall not go far wrong if we look for the reason for its persistence in the face of such a mass of contradictory evidence in the association of the idea—or emotion-idea—of Progress with the pleasure of the really massive and sweeping superiority feelings it liberates in us.

(Those feelings of superiority: we saw how it was to them that the derogating lie owed its swift flight around the earth. But lies that are not belittling but on the contrary flattering to someone whether of our own generation or in history will frequently pass equally swiftly and prove equally insusceptible of being overtaken by truth; and in this case it is the same superiority feelings that are aroused in us and account for the swiftness of their passage from one person to another. In the first instance it is what we may call superiority by distinction: we are able to feel superior by drawing a line between ourselves and the other person —"thank God we are not as this drunkard, or this wanton, or child-murderer or debauchee." In the second instance it is what we may call superiority by identification: we feel superior by identifying ourselves with the other person; we see ourselves in him, and when we admire him we admire ourselves. [No examples here, or we shall have the issue clouded at once by ardent, hostile emotions in ourselves, feeling that our favourite "heroes" are attacked.] It is superiority by identification that is at work also in historical judgments of the joyful acclamation sort, such as we experience in seeing the word, Waterloo. We identify ourselves, because we have been trained to do so, with the winning side, so that it was not only Wellington and "the British" but we also who were "up," and it was in respect of ourselves also that Napoleon and "the French" were "down."
It goes so far that the same name may be the stimulus that sets off both sorts of superiority. When the name Robert Burnes occurs, there occurs also in us the notion "drunkard" and we immediately and most agreeably experience superiority by distinction: we say

"Puir Rabbie!" wagging our heads; in other words, "Thank God I am not as this drunkard." And the superiority is the higher and more gratifying in that the man we are superior to was in his own right a man of incontestable greatness: we are able to feel that mediocrities though we may be we are superior to the greatness of another; the psychological mechanism is that by our "Puir Rabbie!" we lower his greatness in such fashion that *we are able not to feel oppressed by it.* Simultaneously however we may in this case feel also the superiority which comes from identification. Who has not heard or had said to him by someone far from distinguished for his mental parts—and more likely than not in a state of some inebriety—"As Rabbie Burns said, 'A man's a man for aa that!',", clearly interpreting this in private fashion—and quite wrongly—as meaning, "I'm as guid as you—and a damned sight better—and Rabbie Burns, who was a great poet, said so!" So we at the same time patronise Burnes as a drunkard in order to feel superior to *him,* and invoke his greatness so as to have incontestable authority for feeling superior to *others.*

It is only fair to us to say that most—if not all—of this proceeds somewhat below full consciousness. All the same it is high time we knew what goes on in ourselves. There can be no doubt that as things stand at the moment man's chances of even surviving, at any rate as a civilised being and a free personality, hang entirely upon how soon and how widely we come to understand what sort of beings we are and how we work, and what our true motives are, which are the true causes of the state of our world.)

A further—and final—objection to "philosophies of history" such as Progress, and Design- and Pattern-systems in general, is that they may lead directly to inertia. If the course of things is settled in advance anyhow, what need is there for me to exert myself? I can feel justified in giving my mind and my time to my chosen avocations and distractions of whatever sort—while my own particular society and culture, it may be, for want of my activity and that of others like me, reels to destruction. As it was bound to happen anyhow, I cannot be blamed. Alternatively, a "philosophy of history," like Progress itself in its heyday and

Marxism or Dialectical Materialism in our times, by causing the individual to identify himself with the historical process itself, to feel himself a veritable agent of inexorable historical law, is likely to arouse himself to a frenzied activity, dedicated in the case of Marxism to the subversion of the constituted order of his society.

So far as the social organism is concerned, then, doctrines of whatever sort according to which the course of history is fixed in advance can result only in a dangerous and possibly fatal inertia or a frenzy of destructive and potentially disastrous activity.

II

HISTORY IS MAN'S. It is nothing more and can be nothing more than the story of man acting under the influence of whatever he has been influenced by at the time of his action. Where there has been a conflict in history there has been nothing there to decide the conflict except the actual elements of which the conflict has been composed; no invisible Third Party was ever present or ever pushed history in any direction so as to form any Pattern or Design; and the outcome of the conflict is as likely to have been "bad" as "good," retrograde as progressive—insofar as those are even correct or allowable historical terms.

History, then, was in the first instance written only by man. Unfortunately it has been written all over again by historians. And the difference between the two versions has been as large as the individual "historian's" incapacity, ignorance, and conscious or unconscious prejudice or intention to impose his personal view or scheme on the material. Unfortunately in the conditions in which we learned our "history" it is the historian's view—*some* historian's view—and not history itself which we "know"—unless we are exceptionally energetic intellectually, or exceptionally capable of independent critical judgments, or exceptionally endowed with the right quality of historical imagination, or exceptionally fortunate in falling in with the neglected, ignored or unknown fact-material, or exceptionally endowed with that scarcest of gifts, the ability to be aware of ourselves thinking and simultaneously of the emotions the process is evoking and carrying along with it. Very few of us are likely to possess more than one of those qualities in circumstances in which we are free to exercise them, practically no one will be likely to have all together and in equal measure. So history as man wrote it remains unknown, and we to that extent remain deprived of that true knowledge of man which according to Jung can alone avert coming evil.

Of course to some extent or other a personal element in history-writing can never be eliminated. Every mind, even the very largest, has its limitations and those it cannot help but impose on the material it "knows." So that history could not help but be reduced from its full dimensions no matter who wrote it.

What then are we complaining of?

Of insufficient recognition being paid to this fact and insufficient allowance being made for it, of course. But above all of what are demonstrably no more than partial, personal or partisan views, versions, visions or schemes of history which have been and are being imposed under some degree of official sanction in various parts of the earth—indeed in every part of the "educated" earth—with the effect both in past and present of driving men mad with falsehood and setting humanity flamingly at odds together.

What steps are taken and what methods adopted in order to indue whole populations with a desired set of notions with predetermined emotional accompaniments would be a large study in itself and can certainly not be undertaken here. (We are not referring of course to the crude methods of incantatory iteration of catch-phrases and slogans designed to induce mass intoxication, more characteristic of the activities of politicians and journalists across the world, but rather to work of alleged serious purport put forth in the manner of learned or at least judicial history—although even in this, once one is on the look-out for it, one can detect plenty of iterated incantation of a subtle and more hidden sort.) In brief the method has the effect of causing the factual (or fictional) elements of "history" which it is desired the population should "know" to be more real in the mind or solid in consciousness, and consequently more evocative of consent, than other factual elements, *not* desired to evoke consent, which will by comparison be reduced to a less reality in the mind by less frequent mention and in a less affirming or even a subtly derisive tone—the method of Falsification by Inflation on the one hand and a corresponding Falsification by Diminution on the other.

If there is some part of the past which it is particularly desired should not be known at all we may have the Lie by Omission: a particular area of objective historical fact will simply be left out altogether of all histories, simply dropped from mention. Thereby it will have no reality in the individual consciousness and will be as if it had never been: it will have been abolished from its own place in the past and prevented from having any impact on the present through its non-existence in minds.

An interesting example of the Lie by Omission I give by reason of its particular blatancy, as also because it lies directly across my path and illustrates, as will be later seen, an aspect of my thesis.

We may call it a Plain Tale from History.

Before the young king of Macedon set out (in the fourth century B.C.) on that meteoric course of conquest which carried him across half the world and earned for him the title of Alexander the Great, he like a prudent general first secured his rear. This he did by confirming an already long-standing friendship between the Greeks and the people who at that time and for centuries before had been the greatest power in Europe. This was the Keltic Empire which, starting up from its homeland in the heart of what is now Germany, at its greatest extended its boundaries from the Atlantic to the Black Sea; a vast territory held together by political unity and a common language and led by a single king. Greek writers of Alexander's century speak of the Kelts as practising justice and having nearly the same habits and customs as the Greeks. (It may be remembered that in 390 B.C., though they had hitherto been friendly to the Romans, they crushingly defeated them at the Battle of the Allia and a few days later sacked Rome itself as a punishment for what they considered an act of treachery.)

It was only in the third century B.C. that the Kelts seem to have lost their political unity and consequently their hitherto unbroken habit of victory. This may have been in large part due to the revolt of the Germans. Early writers speak only of one people known to them across the mainland of Europe, the Kelts, because they knew of no other. There was another people there, however—the Germans—and their escaping the notice of outside observers was due to their condition of subservience to the Kelts.

That that subservience was long is evidenced by the heavy list of loan words from Keltic which exists in German—while there was no traffic in the other direction.

It is here, in fact, in their philology, that we probably see the reason why the Germans after so many centuries of subjection nevertheless retained their identity and were eventually able to secure their independence. There are no Keltic borrowings among Germanic words for gods or religion, the religious system and customs of the Germans remained different from and unaffected by those of the Kelts, and this fact no doubt explains their survival as a distinct people and their consequent ability in course of time—observe that I avoid saying in due course because "due" carries within it the suggestion of something "right" or "impending in the course of things" and there was of course nothing "right" or "inevitable" or "necessary" about it—simply in course of time, or *as it happened,* the Germanic peoples, round about 300 B.C., were able to throw off the Keltic yoke and establish their independence.

The Keltic territories now were Northern Italy, Gaul or France, Spain or Iberia, the British Isles—and of course Galatia in Asia Minor, where there is direct evidence that Keltic was still spoken for at least another seven hundred years. The Roman conquests to the north and west were conquests of the Keltic lands. What those conquests unquestionably accomplished was the extinction in those territories of the Keltic culture, and very importantly in the event, so to weaken them by the abstraction of native military potential as to leave them defenceless against the wave of invasion by the Germanic tribes when that—as it must have been, frightful event—occurred in the fifth century. Even so the French remain overwhelmingly Latinised Kelt; and in Spain the populations especially of Galicia and Asturias remain of Keltic blood—their most notable gift to mankind being, one imagines, that extraordinary and portentous figure, St John of the Cross.

Help comes from the north, as the ancient Gaelic proverb has it. At no time was it more literally true than after the devastations of wave after wave of Germanic tribesmen right across Western Europe had reduced the towns to ruins and turned great stretches of the once fertile countryside into deserts through

45

the massacre or flight of their populations. From the fifth to the ninth century the brightest light of culture in the West shone from the Keltic parts of the British Isles, and it was sufficient to illumine the darkness of the post-Roman Imperial continent. Generation after generation, band after band of Gaelic missionary monks left their homelands to settle all over the devastated territories, going as far afield as Switzerland and Northern Italy, and carrying on their work of reclamation of the waste and illumination not only of their manuscript books which they did with consummate art and skill but of the minds of the re-attracted and reassembling population.

For centuries this Keltic culture of the British Isles continued to be the brightest area west of Byzantium: one seems to catch a sight of its activity gleaming through the gloom of the barbarism and devastation of those times with the brightness of the colours of its own manuscript illuminations. Then came another shattering example of Progress acting in reverse. The Keltic homelands were themselves attacked and devastated by wave after wave of the most savage yet of all the Germanic tribes—the Norsemen, beside whom the Goths give an impression almost of effeminacy.

Even so, the Gael as it were returned good for evil, pursuing his role of educator and culture-bearer, for it was as a result of contact with his live and exceedingly complex literary development that the saga literature arose and the elaborate poetry of the skalds, which are the glories of Norse culture.

In the meantime the country we call Scotland had coalesced into a kingdom. Before the end of the ninth century the whole country north of the Clyde and Forth had become one; early in the eleventh century the nation had attained practically its historic shape—give and take a few areas of limited extent. It was a Gaelic kingdom. What pockets of pre-Gaelic speech had lingered in what areas and for how long we do not know and shall never know now, and the question is academic. What is unquestionable is that Gaelic gave the nation its unity, and despite the later incursions of Northern English it continued to be the national language and spoken in virtually every part of the country. That it was universally regarded as the national language, the peculiar possession of Scots or Albannaich, spoken by most people or known to have been spoken by practically everyone not so long before, we happen to have the evidence of the two most notable historical writers of the early sixteenth century. Hector Boece and John Major writing separately both witness to the fact that while "Inglis" had been adopted by some of the population, "driven thereto by wars and commerce," Gaelic was still the language of the majority and had been, "not so long ago," the language of the ancestors of nearly all. *And let it be remembered that Gaelic speech meant an extremely high level of both oral and literary culture.* It is valuable to have those authoritative contemporary statements, although in fact the situation they describe might well have been deduced in their absence from what is otherwise known of the persistence of Gaelic in extensive and widely separated areas of Alba or Scotland centuries later.

My point here has not been to "prove" anything, but to prepare the way for a very pertinent question with regard to what we all "know" about history, the view of it that we all more or less carry about with us as defining our position and status in human time, and which we have acquired by direct impregnation during our years at school and by unconscious assimilation during the rest of our life both before and after it, the view which is implicit somewhere or other in practically every piece of printed matter we care to pick up.

The question is this—Those facts that I have stated, the power, duration and dimensions of the Keltic Empire, the unique brilliance of the British-Keltic culture during four centuries following the fall of Rome and the share of the members of that culture in the rebuilding of civilised ways in the devastated areas of the continent, the operation of the same culture in the fertilising of the flower of Norse literature, the formation of a Keltic kingdom of Alba or Scotland whose native, proper and characteristic speech and culture continued to be Gaelic and recognised as such up to the moment when we have chosen to arrest our historical survey, namely half-way through the sixteenth century or thereabouts; those facts are not in dispute or a matter of opinion, they form a perfectly lucid and luminous part of the past: they tell us what all must know if they are to know what the past in our part of the world was like, and moreover in doing so they explain to

47

us who we are—*the question is, why then are they not part of the equipment in consciousness of the people who are the natural heirs of this property in history, culture and tradition?* The facts are accessible, they are more than relevant to, they actually *are* our past, yet they are unknown to us; having regard to the extraordinary tenacity, fullness and fidelity of Gaelic historical and literary tradition (as can still be readily verified) they must have filled and coloured and given its tone to the consciousness of the ancestors of most if not all of us up to the period in question—the mid-sixteenth century—and of a very large proportion for a very long time thereafter; yet they have no existence in and give no tone or colour to the consciousness of ourselves and our contemporaries. One could scarcely encounter a more resounding historical Lie by Omission. *We are like a man upon whom an operation has been performed which has completely destroyed his memory except for the immediate past, so that he remembers what he did yesterday but has no idea who he is or where he came from*—except perhaps that from time to time he may be troubled and disquieted by certain unidentifiable rumours and intimations from behind the curtain of memory. *The question we want to have answered, then, is who performed this operation on us, and how, and to what end?*

It is a question I propose to leave for the moment hanging in the air, for the reason that having arrived at the mid-sixteenth century we have arrived at one of those points in the history of a people when under the influence of new ideas, or at any rate in association with the appearance of new ideas, a great turning is made, old ways are abandoned and the people, whether willingly or otherwise, set off on a new career.

I refer of course to the Reformation.

III

The Reformation

A GREAT MANY books have been written on the Reformation, some of them very weighty indeed, and in more ways than one. One must have read a countless number of them in the course of the last half-century and more. But I must confess to having had, in the case of every one of them, in some degree or other the feeling, as it were, of having "come out by that same door as in I went." Something, one always felt, had been missed—and that something "of the essence."

Many of those books, of course, fall into the category of mere hagiolatry, written by admirers of one or other of the Reformers who could not contain themselves for ardour and had to write a book, or by persons who had to write a book anyhow, no matter for what reason, and knew that in their time the climate of feeling and prevalent preoccupations were such that a book on that subject, written in a certain way, would find a ready market and yield all the rewards of successful authorship. The tone of many of those was venomous and vituperative, but that was not the reason for the residual sense of the "something missed"—a fellow's judgments may be sound although his manners are bad.

Then of course there was the large class of books which dealt in a learned way, with scholarly detachment, or the appearance of it, with the lives of the Reformers, what they did and what they said and their reasons for doing so. The trouble here is that if you write a great many books explaining a person's reasons for doing this or that, you create by implication a very weighty supposition that the cause of his doing this or that was in fact *reasons,* that is, that the causes of his actions arose purely from the rational area of consciousness and were *in fact* such as he described them and himself very probably thought they were. But that, as we all ought to know by now, is a very large and handsome assumption. It is in fact something which is but seldom true of anybody, in any of his actions and activities. In short, what we are given in the large class of those scholarly volumes is what the Reformation was *according to Luther, or Knox, or Calvin,* as elucidated by the learned historian. But that is not what we need to know: what we need to know is what the Reformation was *according to truth*—something which, all possibility of wilful deception set aside, there is a distinct likelihood that Luther, Knox, or Calvin did not clearly know themselves—any more than we ourselves very often know the *causes* of our judgments and actions though we are very fertile in supplying ourselves with *reasons* for them.

That leads us to the attempts that have been made by psychologists to "place" the Reformers in their own categories as cyclothymics, or schizophrenics, or paranoids or what not, and no doubt they are susceptible of being placed if only tentatively in one or the other category if only one knew enough about them; they were after all men of the same stuff as ourselves, and if we can with truth be "placed" in one or other of such categories then given sufficient knowledge about them so could they. My own feeling about men of a certain sour cast of mind, with overtones of gloomy retribution, has always been that they are probably constipated: a good dose of castor oil all round would probably loosen more than their bowels—and I don't by any means intend this facetiously; man is a unity, that's the great point, not a spirit seated in or driving a machine, and there is a highly instructive and deeply helpful doctoral thesis waiting to be written about the correlation between various chemical states of the system and various casts of mind evidenced in various types of opinion and belief, philosophical or religious. But the truth, one fears, would still escape; if the essential *cause* of the Reformation is not described by the external aspect of the Reformers' actions or identical with their doctrines, neither is it to be discerned by the scrutiny of their entrails. One still felt there was something the Reformation *was* which was additional or prior to all this; not unrelated to it, but apart from it.

Then there is the school which interprets the Reformation in social terms, for instance as a movement which liberated the acquisitive elements in society, the frustrated lesser nobility and rich merchants, a movement which, by removing the protective shield of Catholic social doctrine and practice, left the poor unprotected against the rich. That these were the social consequences of the Reformation nobody at this time of day would care to deny: it is plain to be observed in the records of the times (and especially of later times) that the Reformation was, as someone has put it, "a successful revolt of the rich against the poor," and that it signified the appearance on the stage in the leading rôle in the human drama of that portentous figure, the bourgeois. (Let Marxists rejoice—or rather let them not; for it would be premature and out of place. It would be premature because the enlargement of the role and power of the bourgoisie was only a social *effect* of the Reformation, not the Reformation *in se*—in other words just another symptom; and it would be out of place simply because the enlargement of the power of the bourgeoisie was a direct result of the Reformation, *not* of the presence and activity of that superstitiously conceived Third Party, Dialectical Materialism, bustling about in history and for its own ends, unconceived by the actors, pushing events this way and that).

So far we have had the hagiolatrous, the scholarly, the psychological—even the medical—and the social approach. None seems to have penetrated to the root-essence of the matter. Still less does what we may call the political approach. One has heard the Scottish Reformation summed up, for instance, as "a successful stroke of English policy," and that is a perfectly valid statement so far as it takes us. But it doesn't take us very far— no farther than a description of an element in the circumstances surrounding the Scottish Reformation and in the midst of which the event itself, whatever it was, took place. The Reformation would still have been the Reformation had there been no advantage to England—although in that case of course, it would not have succeeded: the point is irrelevant as regards the question we have decided we must concern ourselves with, namely what the Reformation was *in itself,* as an event in the human person, or at any rate in some particular human persons, whether in the conscious or subconscious regions of their personality, in their intellect, their emotions or their will.

After what has been said earlier we need delay very little over the notion or "feeling" that the Reformation was necessary or inevitable according to the ineluctable Law of Progress. For

51

those of us who were brought up in the Reformation tradition this notion or "feeling" is probably the strongest part of our adherence to it. The Reformation simply was something which *had* to happen, it was the "obvious" next step and humanity was waiting for it, it represented an advance of an absolute kind and "Progress" saw that it took place, those who opposed it did so out of perversity and darkness of mind, failing in their obliquity to "see" that "Progress" required it. It is an idea and a feeling that adheres most obstinately in the mind and in the will: relinquishing it would require the abandonment of enormously gratifying feelings of superiority in ourselves and power over our material. By identifying ourselves, as we have grown up to do, with those who brought about the Reformation, we are able to feel ourselves as we suppose them to have been, the veritable agents of ineluctable change, history itself like a great wind passing through us.

It won't do. We are at liberty to admire the Reformers, to accept their doctrines, to regard the Reformation as a good thing to have happened, all as we find good reason. But we are *not* at liberty to regard the Reformation as an example of "Progress" pushing history another step "forward," for that would be to invoke the Third Party Necessarily Present in history and there was no such thing: if the Reformation succeeded in those areas where it did succeed, it was entirely the result of the sufficient effort, method and resources of the individual men concerned, in the circumstances of the insufficient effort, method and resources of their opponents. As to the Reformation's having been inevitable, on the contrary, as in the case of so many revolutions, it was touch-and-go on more than one occasion. It was touch-and-go in Scotland at the time it first succeeded, when English intervention for England's own political purpose turned the scales. And a century after its first outbreaking it was all but rolled up on the continent before the forces of the Counter-Reformation, its rescue there having been by the action of Catholic France which for reasons of its own nationalistic aspirations was ready to support anything at all that helped to diminish the rival power of the Empire. In the pantheon of Leaders and Founders of the Reformation there ought to be a special niche reserved for the Catholic Cardinal Richelieu.

Finally as to the most frequent assertion of all, that the cause of the Reformation was the morals of the clergy—was I as a schoolboy afflicted with precocity of the logical faculty, or have many others also sensed the colossal non-sequitur in the suggestion made to us that because (it was alleged) the *morals* of the pre-Reformation clergy were bad, therefore the *doctrines* of the Reformers were true? Logically that is as sound as to say that eggs being four shillings a dozen, *therefore* it is twenty miles to Inverness. John Smith may be able to show that James Brown is a thief; that would only mean that James Brown is in need of becoming honest, it could never be taken as a proof that John Smith's opinions are true on politics or any other subject than the morals of James Brown—which don't in any case concern him. In short the entire question as to the morals of the clergy in the sixteenth century is irrelevant and immaterial as to the question of the theological truth of Protestant dogma.

As it is irrelevant and immaterial we shall have to leave it aside, only to say that it is by no means accepted that those morals were as they were painted by the Reformers. I think it was the late G. K. Chesterton who said. "Nobody noticed the monks were lazy until they coveted their possessions." Granted that sixteenth-century society, even clerical society, was not perfect and contained scandals—there has never been a human society that didn't—the picture the Reformers drew of those they aspired to supplant was probably about as true as the Soviet posters showing bloated "capitalists" devouring "workers" are representative of actual conditions in the non-Communist world; about as true as taking the columns of the *News of the World* as an authentic picture of actual contemporary British society, or as making the sum total of gangster stories equal the social life of the United States of America.

The point is worth making *in extenso* in the interests of historical truth and by way of getting our facts in focus. But in another context. Here we can no longer delay taking up the question we found confronting us when we reached the mid-sixteenth century—what was this event which suddenly arrived in Scotland (and elsewhere) and turned the whole nation and people out of their historic course and set them off in a different direction? What in fact *was* the Reformation—that is, *in itself*—

what was "the thing" that happened, the event in persons? A question to which hagiolators, scholarly apologists, psychologists, sociologists, men of medicine, historians of politics, all appear to have given only incomplete answers, valid—if valid at all—only within their own "terms of reference."

IV

THE QUESTION was a very personal one for me, and from my earliest years. Indeed my first awakenings to consciousness of self-hood appear to me in retrospect to have taken place in the shadow of the Reformation. Memories of infancy are of course notoriously coloured by later experience and not to be relied on. It happens however that I am able to be sure about a particular date. When I was three years of age my maternal grandfather died, and that event brought about a change of residence for us; so that anything I remember from that first house and street must have taken place before I was four.

Now already at that age I was aware of "something," some "influence" from outside myself invading my consciousness: *as if some pattern from outside were endeavouring to superimpose itself on the pattern of my natural or primary impulses.*

There is a picture. I am standing in a garden, entranced by a vision of flowers: it might have been the first time I had "seen" flowers. At any rate I am rooted to the spot by a sense of the glory all around me. I am bending towards one bloom, breathless in the blaze of its reality and being, when from behind my back comes a loud peremptory and admonitory rapping on a window pane. I recognise it of course at once and become rigid: it is this "influence" from "outside" which has always come between me and my responsive affirmations. And it is as if a shadow fell at that moment over the flower, hiding its glory of *being* or diminishng it in the bloom itself before my eyes.

This might be a composite recollection, constructed in part out of later material—as I say, memories from infancy are notoriously unreliable. No matter. The picture will stand absolutely as an accurate description of how I experienced this something from outside myself which persisted in making claims to authority over my world within: *I felt it as something blurring if not inhibiting the spontaneity of my affirmative responses to what was not-myself.*

I appeared to be subject to two laws or authorities which

were in opposition the one to the other, one from within which was right and yet I was given to understand was wrong and one from without which in terms of my nature was wrong and yet, it appeared, was right. It deeply disturbed me as a child and it continued to perplex me as I grew up—long after I had identified the authority-from-without as the law of our Religion, whose authority emanated in turn from the Black Books (printed on thin, fine paper which it was a—one felt sure prohibited—sensual joy to finger) which were everywhere about the house, constantly in use, and could be seen protruding from the side pockets of every visitor. (We were a tight, small, utterly exclusive society of the most extreme Evangelicals; holding the sort of religion that was all but universal in Scotland several centuries ago. This was in its way an advantage for anyone who hoped later on to come to terms of comprehension with the Reformation episode, since it meant that I was compelled to experience at first hand and in my most impressionable years what this religion had really been like all the way back to sub-Reformation and—with the exception of course of the element of public violence—even Reformation times. It is a privilege few have today: if many people had it there would be a clearer vision about the thing: as it is most of us have no knowledge of it, only strong feelings about it.)

I early came to realise that the law from outside, rapping peremptorily on the window-pane, was *Truth,* and the inner law of my being which it interrupted and rebuked, was *Sin.* I apprehended that the Truth was the Shadow on the Rose, as I had felt it in the garden—the Shadow on the Rose of the whole World, one might say, since it pursued me tenaciously into the larger levels of experience. *Sin was in the Answering of my spirit to the Rose*—perhaps even *in the rose itself.* Since the Truth that came from without came with very great, indeed undisputed authority (since no one not of our community ever entered the house), and the Sin that came from within arose in my case at any rate with very great, indeed uncontrollable force, one can see that I had a first-class personal problem, a conflict in consciousness re-enlivened or generated afresh in every moment of experience.

Eventually, unsatisfied by what seemed the only partial truth arrived at by the different methods of approach already mentioned, I sat down, some quarter of a century ago or more, determined if it should be possible to think my way through to the one thing that seemed to have been missed, the essential thing, that which the Reformation had been *in itself*, irrespective of adhering conditions of place and time—it having been very early made clear to me, I need hardly say, that the "Truth," our very pure Evangelical religion, had descended to us from, or in the language of the time, had been *won for us* by, the Reformation: (even at this late day, at the phrase "won for us by the Reformation" my associated, conditioned emotions shout hurrah, hurrah, hurrah! in me. I ignore them, because they are not, and are incapable of ever being, a judgment).

The method I adopted was that of a novel of the dramatic type, in which the characters, representing the various elements involved in the Reformation in Scotland, acted and reacted upon each other and so wove a pattern of events which ought to have described the course of the movement and, one hoped, displayed its nature. The danger of such a method is obvious; it is that the author will without realising it involve himself in the action, that he will conduct his characters through the action of the play instead of leaving them to work it out themselves according to their proper natures, that he may have wrongly conceived those natures in the first place—in short that in one way or another he ends by finding in his book what he himself has first put into it.

It is a danger which is bound to be less the more its presence is realised. I am speaking of course of a novel used as a method of enquiry, not of a novel written to a thesis, that is, designed of set purpose to illustrate and lead up to conclusions consciously present in the author's mind before he began to write the book. No such thing was the case with me, for while before I began I may have had some idea of the general direction in which the movement was likely to drift, *I had as it turned out no idea at all, no idea whatever, at what I was to arrive*: so much so that when I did arrive I was totally astounded at where I found myself. If I am right in my conclusions where I found myself was not particularly in the sixteenth century at all, or in any particular century, or any particular country, but right in the homeland of basic human motivation in all times, among basic human motivations of any time or any place *right where they reside,* and that therefore what I had so unexpectedly "turned-up" appertained to nothing less than that knowledge of man which alone, according to Jung, can dispel the shadow of coming evil.

I was very naive of course if I ever expected that novel to be published as a novel. The days are long gone by when the public will tolerate being edified by a novelist, or indeed being edified at all by any kind of writer. Writers no longer lead public opinion. All the same it is a pity the novel could not have appeared because its not having done so means that I am pretty well bound down here to presenting my conclusions without having sufficiently prepared for them. Manifestly those conclusions if they are valid at all are valid irrespective of the merit or success of the method used to arrive at them, that is, through the means of a dramatic novel: one can take a wrong or devious route and still arrive, even if only by chance, at the right destination. All the same one would have wished for space in which to develop the argument because the conclusions if they are indeed valid seem to be of such a kind as to show practically all writing about the Reformation up till now as having been in varying degree beside the point.

That is a tall claim, but the conclusions have been standing there in the mind for years, under constant re-examination by an eye zealous for truth, without a single crack having been discovered in their monolithic presence.

Great care had to be taken, of course, to see that the *personae* of the drama were real persons—not puppets or mere "characters" —and correctly motivated: there were various characteristics in the main *personae* of which one could be reasonably, or fairly, or even quite certain, before letting them loose to act on one another. With lesser characters there was less difficulty—the member of the smaller nobility, for instance, who didn't care a hank of tow for theological points but was in it for what he could get, in this case the landed wealth of the neighbouring priory: such types infest most societies more or less, and while as representing the element of simple avarice he might have been a leading actor in a drama intended to explain—that is, to explain away—the Reformation in terms of social changes, in a drama intended to work down to the ultimate motivation or deepest springs of the Reformation as an event in actual human persons, he merited little more than a walking-on part: he was not really an actor in the drama, he merely happened to be present at the time it worked itself out, and took part in the action only insofar as he saw the opportunity for furthering his private aims, so that he was more a part of the setting in time and place than a part of the drama itself. It is true that the Reformers could not have become the "winning side" in Scotland or anywhere but for their alliance with that "unprincipled pack of famished hyenas" as Carlyle called the nobility, but once they had together become the winning side it was the doctrines, the "mind" of the Reformers which was enforced upon succeeding generations so as to become their unquestioned view upon life, and it was that "mind" of the Reformers therefore which was the essence of the Reformation and must be the subject of enquiry.

—One very important historical point requires to be made before we can proceed. If we watch what we are doing when we think about the Reformation we shall see without difficulty that we are thinking of it as if it had been a contest between two "sides," "the Catholics" and "the Protestants," somewhat like a football match played out on the "field" of the sixteenth century before an audience of posterity containing "supporters" of either "side." This is a bad example of falsification by simple dual-categorising of the material and as a view is totally unhistorical. It was not like that at all at the time. The Reformers and their supporters may have formed a "side," but there was no such "side" as "the Catholics." What we call "the Catholics" were simply Europe, in other words, Christendom. Europe, Christendom, the Church, were practically interchangeable terms, and had been so for a millennium. Europe had grown up by, with and in the Church, which had been the generating element of the vast and sustained social, intellectual and moral effort which produced the "Thing" that was Europe, a varied and diverse society which was nevertheless One Thing, with common intellectual, moral and social ideals, a common "mind" upon life, and a common language of culture and intellectual activity. It was this Unity of life and traditions which the Reformers set out to overthrow, in order to replace it—not by freedom of choice in religion: such a notion was never conceived—but by their own governance: in Scotland in particular the sect of Calvinists claimed nothing less than that the civil power itself should be directly subject to their supervision and control.

It is rank bad history therefore to think of the Reformation as a contest between two "sides"—the "baddies," of course, and the "goodies"—and as long as we think of it in those terms we shall never understand it. It would be correctly thought of in terms of an historic city full of magnificent buildings and with enormously much to its credit as a lamp to the countryside, suddenly attacked by a ferocious enemy bent purely on its destruction. That this enemy thought they had a mandate from God to destroy the city is beside the point: for the moment what was going on inside their heads is not the question, which is simply the historical "picture" of events.—

That point having been made, let us return to the book. The main tension in the drama centred about two priests, two of the secular or parish clergy, who had known each other most of their lives from their seminary days, and at the first rising of the curtain are resident together under the same roof, in the same manse or presbytery; one of whom was to become a Reformer, the other not. The question was, why?

The answer can only have lain somewhere in the inner world of the two protagonists. For even if it be assumed that the doctrines of the Reformers were self-evidently true, there must still have been some reason why one of those two was able to perceive this, while the other was not—I am of course stipulating that both were in good faith throughout; to suppose anything else would be to ruin the experiment and make its conclusions meaningless by the introduction of an unknown factor which could not be controlled. What then are the personality or other characteristics which can with certainty or at the very least plausibility be distributed between those two, bearing in mind what position each is to take up, which we know in advance?

In a priest of the sixteenth century who was to become a Reformer there must have been a pre-existing conflict or at least disequilibriated condition in the personality which the embracing of Protestantism resolved or promised to resolve. We can be sure of such a person at least that prior to his encountering Protestantism he must have sat to some extent uncomfortably with himself and in the conditions of his age and place, perhaps in his condition in society.

To account for such a condition in him I made this priest to have started life as the over-protected and over-indulged only son of the widow of a well-to-do merchant, and described the severe emotional shock he received on passing from his domestic environment, where his will had been paramount and his whim law, to the school or seminary, where among boys at the merciless stage of life his lordly ways and attempts to take the lead and impose his will earned him only resentment and antagonism. In the circumstances of his upbringing and his personal characteristics he was in fact predestined to be a butt. Boys will not tolerate pretentiousness and lordliness, least of all in one who is physically unimpressive and otherwise ungifted. John Tod could shine at nothing, not at their sports and games for he was of an insignificant physique, not at their studies for though he applied himself with assiduity his talents, it soon appeared, were mediocre. Those who would nonetheless have taken him up out of kindliness soon found him too demanding in personal relationships and kept clear. So he was isolated with his resentment and the distress of not being able, no matter in what direction he tried, to compel the world outside him to accept him at the lordly valuation his first and formative environment had accorded him and which he was bound to feel ever after was his real due, what was owed to him by life. This then was the source of *his* particular unease and disequilibrium, and it followed that he would be quite unconsciously seeking for something which would be the means of his re-ascending to his original sense of fulfilment and pre-eminence.

He was not entirely without means to assert himself even so. He was striking-looking, in spite of his small stature, by reason of his shock of fiery hair, contrasting with the even, pale complexion that goes with it, and—his most striking feature—a remarkable pair of burning brown eyes. When he was in a state of inner excitement or tension, which was usual, they *glowed*. Normally, as he felt the world's hostility he kept them lowered, which in some quarters, in spite of his consequential strut, earned him a reputation for humility. But from time to time he would lift them up upon a person with such a baleful glow like malice or resentment as made the other uneasy and if he was speaking fall silent. His greatest asset of all however was in the possession of a voice of quite exceptional power combined with a torrential flow of words. He had discovered its use in the seminary as a weapon of defence from the time when, driven into a corner and with no way of escape, he had suddenly lifted it up in full throat and called down curses and maledictions in grisly multitude on his persecutors. On that occasion they had drawn back in astonishment and consternation, some even crossing themselves and looking at him askance, and from then on even the boldest among them took care not to irritate him beyond a certain point. His nickname, both at the seminary and ever afterwards, was "the Prophet."

As a priest he was both enormously fulfilled and agonisingly tormented—without, it is understood, having the least notion why in either case. In all that concerned his pastoral function of preaching, exhorting and admonishing he could be his first unfrustrated, uninhibited self: he came into his own. Of the most conspicuous rectitude in his own life, he came to be feared, and not only among the laity, for the severity of his strictures, and they were incessant, upon the transgressions of everyone else—or simply upon transgressions in general. On the other hand, the exercise of his sacrificial function never failed to afflict him with a mysterious, unnamed terror. Standing before the Altar, holding the Body of Christ in his hands, or at the words of Consecration, he would become rigid with some fear as of annihilation, feel unable to proceed, and as he could not flee away physically fled away inside himself—a "fama" of his holiness began to spread abroad because of his supposed habitual mystical entrancement standing there in body while his spirit was away. . . .

In the novel of course all this had not to be *told,* but *shown,* or *conveyed.* As for instance almost at the beginning there is a midnight Mass at Christmas. First there is a poetic passage intended to convey the joy and peace in hearts because it is Christmas, the silence and expectation in the church as the Mass begins. Then . . . John Tod has mounted to the pulpit. When he uncovers his head it seems in its brightness to add one to the company of the angels under the roof and the saints standing in their niches.

The Gospel of the Mass is taken from the Holy Gospel according to Saint Luke, chapter two: Joseph went up from Galilee to Bethlehem in Judea with Mary his espoused wife, and her days being accomplished she brought forth her first-born son and wrapped him in swaddling clothes and laid him in a manger: and the angel of the Lord appeared to shepherds watching their sheep and said to them: Fear not, for behold I bring you good tidings of great joy, that shall be to all the people, for this day is born to you a Saviour, which is Christ the Lord. But John Tod takes his text from the Lesson of the Mass, which is from the Epistle of Saint Paul the Apostle to Titus, chapter two: The grace of God our Saviour hath appeared to all men, instructing us, that denying ungodliness and worldly desires, we should live soberly, and justly and godly in this world.

Ungodliness and worldly desires! He seems immediately to become incensed with somebody, and in the sound of his trumpeting the dew of peace is turned into a rain of wrath. The indignation in his voice returns to him quivering from the walls and roof, and makes him in turn indignant. He soars upwards on it. Out of the partial gloom the faces are turned attentively, riveted by a voice, and the voice is his. The sound, though it fill the building, is no greater than his swelling consciousness. He rises with its volume till he is become no common vessel, but a man "sent." He sees his warrant in their paling faces. They are compelled to listen—cannot not listen—to his thunder, while he plays upon them like an organ. As the roof resounds the more, he rises more unlimited, and calls forth on them the greater loudness of a paler hue. Till when he feels them shudder his unfettered being floats upon the sounding air.

He is descending now from the pulpit, passes, dipping, before the Altar, vests, is conducted back, all as in a dream. And in the o'erhang of a dream he mounts the Altar and begins the Creed.

But now as he proceeded with that part of the Mass called the Offertory the vapour of his dream began to waver and be blown upon by a never yet identified anticipation. There was some reluctance, not to be shaken off; his hands above the Altar were growing heavy. The ringing of a bell at his back evoked a sickness and anxiety, and immediately the urgency of an impulse took the form of thinking he heard feet—his own feet—retreating in a panic scamper. His hands had become like lead.

"For—this—is—My—Body."

He had cast himself headlong down before the Altar, hiding his face, striving to grovel from sight, while he cried out, "Holy, holy, holy!" with shrieks and smitings of the breast. At the same time and with absolute simultaneity he was flying backwards, pushing out his hands before him, crying, "I cannot, I cannot!"— then rushing out of the building struggling against some weight of being that pressed upon him, threatening to crush him utterly to nothing. . . . In reality he was standing still before the Altar, shaken and oblivious; in the hush of the elements listening to the storm, mounting up, shrieking, blotting out the world.

Presently he knew where he was, and what in act of doing. But still the tempest raged apace, and was suddenly injected with a stream of intemperate feeling from below, staining all other components of the conflict with a red like fury. The end was that he finished saying Mass with his mind averted from the meaning of all he said and did—yet as it were averting it from that averting of it. So strong and insuperable the tension in him of strange contending opposites that he could scarcely tell whether he bowed when he ought to bow or retained himself erect: sometimes it even seemed that he did both at once.

As he came from the Altar he saw nothing of the people standing. He was wrapped away. A sense was in him as of sacrilege, a guilty awe: at the same time a sense of deprivation, of having been robbed. And mingled with them—and rising to the mastery—a burning deep resentment.

I ought at this point to enter a caveat lest anyone should be tempted to think this person of the drama had been composed merely of characteristics thrown together at haphazard, or to serve some unavowed purpose of the author's own to represent the priest-who-was-to-turn-Reformer in a certain way. On the contrary, there is sound authority for every one of them—except the flaming hair, a novelist's gratuitous decoration. He had to have a conflict in the personality, or there would have been nothing for the vision of the truth of the new doctrines to resolve; and my means of inducing such a conflict were as plausible as I could think of; had I been able to think of any more plausible I'd have used them. His small stature was statistically necessary; practically all—if not indeed all—leaders of revolutionary movements aimed at the violent overthrow of the established order have been small men, or at any rate men of low stature. (The converse does not hold, of course. Revolutionaries are small men does not mean that small men are revolutionaries, actual or potential. Far from it: many of the "biggest" men of history, of the most affirmative cast of mind, who have contributed most in a positive way to their times—and not only their own times—have been small in stature. The names of Ludwig van Beethoven, Ignatius of Loyola, Francis of Assisi or for that matter Saul of Tarsus do not bring to mind the epithet "small," but rather "majestic" or even "colossal." But that the leadership of violent revolutionary movements aimed at overthrowing the established order is composed of men of low stature is also true. We have an excellent example to hand in *the* Revolution of our own times. Marx, Lenin, Trotsky, Stalin, Molotov, Khrushchev . . . one can run through the entire list of the leaders of the first forty years of Communism and it is almost without exception a row of dwarfs.) The point is not essential to my thesis: I do say however that faced with the necessity of apportioning physical characteristics between two men in the situation of my chief actors, likelihood more than demanded that the small man should be the revolutionary. I leave unassessed in this context the question as to the part played by poor physique in conditioning the subject to resentment and an attitude of generalised aggressiveness by way of compensation for a sense of physical inadequacy.

Equally there can be no question of the rightness of the resounding voice, the torrential eloquence, the passion for censure and admonition, threat and malediction, the enormous emotional force. Luther and Knox were typical in this respect: each was "a volcanic emotional force without any counterbalancing power of intellect." For John Tod's intellectual mediocrity was entirely typical too. We may claim if we care that it was a case of God having "hid those things from the wise and prudent and revealed them unto babes." What is unquestionable is the truth of G. K. Chesterton's statement that "on the great map which is the intellect of St Thomas Aquinas, the mind of Luther would be an invisible point," and it has been not once but many times pointed out that a principal significance of the Reformation is that it was "a revolt of the will against the intellect." We may if we care agree with the anti-intellectual attitude, but we cannot deny that it was there, and very deeply and essentially there, in the Reformation movement, so much so that it gives that movement its peculiar "mark" or "note," which it had from its leaders and has retained ever since. Some of Luther's strongest outbursts were against the faculty of Reason—as someone has said, "Luther's outbursts against the Reason were nothing short of ferocious; not even the Pope inspired in him such vituperation"—as for example in his last Wittenberg sermon where he exclaimed: "Reason is a whore! Reason is the Devil's greatest whore! Does the Reason give light? Yea, verily, like the light filth would give forth if it were put in a lantern."

Lastly, John Tod's terror and recoil in his sacrificial function is also in the authentic tradition. Luther notably exhibited profound emotional disturbance in similar case, even on one occasion at least to falling down in a fit before the altar—(his emotional aversion extended even to crucifixes and representations of Christ: he said of his time as a monk, "I had such an aversion for Christ that when I saw one of his images, for example the crucifix, I at once felt terrified; I would more willingly have seen the devil.")

So we have sound historical justification for every one of the elements of which we composed the personality of the priest who was to turn Reformer. The other, who was to be unattracted by the Reformation, was much easier to characterise. I had only to make him as he was bound to have been, at ease with himself, his circumstances and his age. I made him large and fair, a thoroughly "normal" man, with a normal and this time rural upbringing among brothers and sisters. Coming from rural Ayrshire he differed from John Tod in having Scottish or Gaelic as his native language—(with the exception of George Buchanan, who was born within sight of Glasgow, all the Reforming leaders and practically all their adherents came from the "Scots" or English speaking minority). In calling him Kennedy I had in mind not only the part of the country he came from but no doubt also in particular the Ayrshire Gaelic poet of the previous generation, Walter Kennedy, and also Quintin Kennedy, the Abbot of Crossraguel, who years later confuted the Reformers, both Knox and Willock, in controversy. He was of as even and "warm" a disposition as his friend John Tod was alternately frigid and tempestuous, a scholar and teacher and a man of high intelligence—he had to be because he was required to argue to some purpose later—so that in giving him the first name Ringean or Ninian I doubtless had in mind Ninian Winyet, the schoolmaster of Linlithgow, whose publications following the Reformation's success Knox suppressed and whose repeated challenges to public debate he either could not or would not meet—otherwise than with a posse of soldiers sent to wreck his printers.

The opening scene in the book showed the contrast in personality conditions. It opened seconds after a frightful piece of news had been received by the two men, so that they were sitting at either side of a table, each equally numbed with shock. The news had been that of the assassination of Cardinal Beaton.

Here an effort has to be made to apprehend what the circumstances were in which that particular piece of news produced precisely that effect. It can be done if we keep in mind that what *we* "know" of Cardinal Beaton is only his legend, and that his contemporaries did not know this legend, *for the reason that it had not yet been invented.* It was the product of a later imagination: Cardinal Beaton's unpopularity, like his lolling on cushions to enjoy the spectacle of the "gentle martyr" George Wishart's sufferings in the flames is as historical as Macbeth's colloguing with witches or for that matter his "murder" of the "aged" King Duncan, which never took place. What Cardinal Beaton's contemporaries reacted to therefore was quite simply what his assassination really meant in terms of the facts of the then situation, which were perfectly well and only too painfully realised by them.

The facts were that Scotland was at that moment in danger as perhaps never before. The English King, Henry VIII, was pursuing his claims to what he called "the ownership of Scotland" by the most openly genocidal methods. Army after English army was being despatched north over the border under his express orders to slaughter every Scot of any age and either sex and to burn and destroy every building from abbey to hovel. To make matters inconceivably worse a large if uncertain section of the nobility, living up to Carlyle's description of them as an "unprincipled pack of famished hyenas," was known to be in English pay. The situation was more than desperate, and in this situation the whole hopes and confidence of the Scottish nation rested upon one man, the Chancellor of the Kingdom, Cardinal Beaton, who alone was known to be immune to either threats or bribes and so astute a statesman as to be capable of countering every one of the English King's moves. His removal therefore, from the point of view of the English King's ambition, was imperative. His murder, then, was at the time perfectly well understood to be what it was, *purely and simply a political assassination.* (The whole story of the haggling that went on as to the price that was to be paid for the deed is plain to be read in the English State Papers of the time—all except the actual amount eventually paid, which page has been removed by that anti-historian, "an unknown hand.") To all Scots not of the small faction in English pay what it amounted to was that by that act the edifice of Scottish nationhood and independence had had its main prop kicked away. The effect must have been something similar to that of an earthquake —the sense of being unmanned, of not knowing where to look for security, especially of not knowing what is still to come, and when and from what direction. Such a sense of shock, bewilderment, panic was experienced throughout Scotland wherever the news of the Cardinal's murder penetrated. The roof of the edifice of Scottish nationhood was felt to tremble. John Tod and Ninian Kennedy felt that first reaction too: they were in those first moments stunned beyond words.

Then a very strange thing happened. In the midst of his stunned horror John Tod startled *himself* by suddenly leaping to his feet and exclaiming, "The douncome!" and again, in his great voice, *"the douncome!"* Why did he do so? *He* didn't know. I'm not sure that as yet I knew myself. It was simply that from the listening post I maintained in his emotions and nerves, and sighting along the course of his future which was known to me though as yet hidden from him, such a rising-up from the sub-rational, sub-conscious area in his personality of a powerful emotion which could have characterised itself at such a moment in the exclamation "the douncome" arose naturally from his internal situation and conflict, was logical and even necessary, in the sense that such a sub-rational, sub-conscious impulse could be perceived in projecting itself forward to link up with certain overt and conscious acts of his later life which had to take place if he was to become a Reformer.

I omit here, because considerations of space so demand, the succeeding section in the novel in which I strove to convey John Tod's distraction in endeavouring to understand his inward state and the elements of the conflict he was aware of in himself, an element of which had become vocal and announced its presence and as it were *almost* disclosed its nature in that incomprehensible shout, "the douncome." It is a pity it could not all have been given. Because what should have been seen to emerge naturally and clearly out of the personality situation is in danger of appearing to jump on to the page looking crude and contrived.

The next section was designed to assist the imagination to project itself into the actual conditions of the times, to convey what it was actually like to live in Alba in those days, and was in effect a description, almost an animated painting, as well as a sound film, done with the utmost realism or naturalism, of one of the many English invasions, beginning with the lighting of the beacons, the hosting of the Scots through the night, and the full-scale battle next day, with the treachery and desertion of most of the nobility on the field. John Tod was present throughout both as priest and soldier, although in fact, thanks to an unfortunate experience in boyhood already elsewhere conveyed, he was very nervous of the military arm. Accordingly when this section was separately published (as *Scottish Noël*) I discarded him for the occasion and replaced him with another priest of identical outward appearance but very different military instincts.

V

On the last day of July 1562 the Protestant Magistrates of Edinburgh with a troop of soldiers attacked the shop of John Scot, printer and publisher in Edinburgh, destroyed his stocks, arrested his person and would have arrested Ninian Winyet (their main objective) except that being unknown to them by appearance he was able to walk out just as they arrived and make his escape. All this was because Winyet had repeatedly challenged Knox to public debate on the Reformers' doctrines and authority, challenges which Knox was either unwilling or unable to accept, and John Scot had printed them.

Four hundred years later almost to the day, in August 1962, there took place in a building scarcely a mile from where this episode had occurred, a formal, public disputation on the original Protestant doctrines and their Scriptural authority—and in an only partially modernised version of the language in which the original debates would have been carried on had they taken place.

For four hundred years it has been thought and taught in Scotland that the Reformers completely vanquished their opponents in plain, fair argument at the time, and that nothing has been heard of argument since because in fact their opponents had nothing to say, "not a leg to stand on." The contrary was the truth. Whenever the Reformers could be brought to fair, plain argument (without, that is, adding military force or mob violence to their theological case) they were vanquished on their own ground, and nothing has been heard of argument on the then issues since, bcause for four hundred years all such argument has been suppressed, simply never allowed to reach the public. So far as I know my playlet-disputation, *Ane Tryall of Heretiks*, was the first occasion for four hundred years when free and public discussion of the Reformers' doctrines was possible or permitted. (As it was, and as if to repeat the historical episode, the Protestant Magistrates of Edinburgh again intervened, this time by a posse of policemen, to close the debate at midnight on Saturday, and prevent its taking place on Sunday at all: apparently not so much on the grounds that the discussion of religion was out of place on a Sunday as that its being done in the form of a formal disputation open to the public made it rank as a form of art-expression).

I give the whole text along with the Foreword here because I cannot evade doing so: it is the next and inevitable step in our argument. For this reason, that if we are to have any success in coming at an understanding of the mind and inward state of the Reformers it is *essential* first of all to have a clear grasp of the doctrines in which they believed they perceived truth.

Ane Tryall of Heretiks

FOREWORD

This is the second chapter of the novel set in the 16th century of which my book published separately as *Scottish Noël* was the first.

That novel was an attempt to work down to the *deep* causes of the volcanic episode designated the Reformation, with the intention that it should perhaps be less the occasion of inherited and uncritical passion and emotion by being the better *understood*. Even at the stage of writing this second chapter I had arrived at the critical judgment that *the doctrines of the Reformers were not identical with the causes of the Reformation*—all non-theological and co-incidental causes apart. Nonetheless the doctrines were unquestionably in the midst of the controversy, so that even if they were not identical with the causes they were manifestly in some way closely connected with them. I considered it necessary therefore before proceeding any further to state plainly what at least the most radical among those doctrines were. A generation or two ago this would not have been necessary: in my Evangelical childhood the doctrines were a matter of continual enunciation in meetinghouse and family circle alike and universally known. Changed days, however; nowadays even in practising Protestant circles the doctrines basic to the Reformers' case are hardly known at all anywhere, certainly not clearly. It was necessary at this point therefore to state them, and state them plainly, before the examination could with any profit be proceeded with; to state them in such a way, in other words, that a reader of the book could not but go forward with a clear and firm grasp of them.

For this a footnote, or even an appendix, would not have sufficed—for the simple reason that no-one as a rule bothers to read them. What was obviously necessary, therefore, was to devise a means of stating the doctrines *as a part of the action of the book,* so that a reader would be unable to avoid acquiring a clear grasp of them while at the same time the action would not only not be held up but even, if it could be contrived, advanced. Accordingly in the end I adopted the device of presenting a contemporary trial for heresy, which would allow the formal statement of the new doctrines, which could be given in the actual words of Luther and Calvin, set over against the Catholic doctrines that stood in refutation of them.

Immediately, of course, the problem arose that the doctrines on either side would have to be presented by *persons:* persons therefore had to be constructed, and they had to be *true* persons, persons, that is to say, such as the protagonists on either side would actually have been at that time. So far as the heretics were concerned that presented few problems: they were, in fact, as they displayed themselves in their own writings, their own descriptions of their acts and attitudes, unquestionably such persons, I think, as I have described them. With their opponents the problem was not so easy. The unsupported evidence of a man's enemies—the more in proportion as they are violent enemies—can never be uncritically accepted as a witness to his character, and the true image of the Scottish mediæval cleric had obviously to be sought and discerned behind the distortions of extreme prejudice which alone have been presented for our acceptance ever since the Reformation triumphed. Let it be pointed out, of course, that there was no question of "making out a case" for the mediæval cleric as a sort of accidental or incidental buttress to the doctrines he was defending: that would be as illicit as what in fact has always been the practice of "proving" the Reformation by reference to the supposed or alleged character of pre-Reformation clerics (it is astonishing that the illicit nature of such a proof should never seem to have been obvious, since there clearly can be no possible progression in logic from the moral character of mediæval clerics to the theological truth of Reformation doctrines). Nor was it even a question of a vindication (although in fact we owe as much in justice to the dead as to the living, and nothing can absolve us from the responsibility attaching to our constant practice of passing retrospective judgments on insufficient evidence or none, in the course of building up some historical "view" which it suits or pleases us to hold). It was quite simply a question of presenting characters which were in fact true to the times and to human nature. Now, just as it is indisputable that there were pre-Reformation bishops who— and on more than one count—were unworthy of their office, it is equally beyond question that there were others of distinguished piety, unquestioned rectitude and illustrious learning. As I could only present one bishop, who had to be as it were a cross-section of the episcopate of the times, it seemed, all due allowances made, that it was in general fair and "true" to present a bishop characterised by undisputed irregularities in his early life who was nevertheless at the time in question eminently worthy of his office. (On the whole question of the morals of the pre-Reformation clergy, having regard to all the evidence, and especially to the fact, true in all times, that evil makes a noise in the world while good tends to go unnoticed, I have seen no reason to doubt the truth of the Bishop's statement in the present text—the words were acually those of King James V—that "*while some* (clergy) *be bad, yet there be mony guid*".)

On one point at least there was historically no question of his "truth": the Bishop was, in common with the entire class of pre-Reformation clergy, of an indomitable and unquenchable patriotism; so that it is exceptionally apt that he should preside over a trial of heretics while still only partially recovered from wounds received in actively repelling the brutal and unprovoked English invasion described in the previous chapter ("Scottish Noël").

A further essential point concerned the attitude in general of the ecclesiastical authorities of the time towards heresy and heretics personally. This had obviously to be authentic. In the first place one had to reject the picture that has been handed down to us of a set of sadists deliberately and consciously destroying, in the cruellest fashion they could devise, men who represented Obvious Truth. It would be difficult to find a worse example of the crucial fallacy of reading history backwards. The ecclesiastical authorities of the day did not and could not have seen in the heretics of their particular time the men of Truth, any more than they could have seen in them the men of the Future. No-one could have anticipated at that time that the heretics of the day were going, by English help, of course, to win complete victory: that must have been still an inconceivable possibility. Moreover all the evidence shows that the authorities were not in Scotland particularly of a persecuting disposition: they were, in fact, rather lax and lackadaisical in putting into action the civil laws which were laid down against heresy of any kind. At the actual time I believe I have been absolutely correct in displaying the attitude of the clerics towards the heretics whom the law required them to try as one above all of general puzzlement and irritation—irritation, if on occasion some amusement, at what seemed the absurdity and baselessness of their contentions, and puzzlement at the reasons for their persistence in adhering to them, especially in view of the penalties the Civil Power then enacted for such public persistence. Moreover the truth is that in Scotland the ecclesiastical authorities, on whom the onus rested of establishing the heresy, were not only not eager, still less ferocious, in the pursuit of suspected persons, but even rather lax and reluctant in the whole matter, so that a holder of heretical opinions was scarcely likely to be taken up so long as he remained quiet and refrained from actively allying himself with treasonable political factions and participation in the most violent sort of breaches of public peace—to say nothing of sacrilege, as in the destruction of ecclesiastical edifices; so that the Bishop in the Tryall was acting perfectly in character, even though from the Civil point of view somewhat straining legality, in endeavouring to avoid outright condemnation of the heretic in question on condition of his undertaking to remain quiet till he came to better reason.

As to the puzzlement of the clerics of the time at the persistence of the heretics in adhering to their doctrines after their untenability had been shown, it will, I hope, be noted how, towards the end, the Bishop begins to have an inkling of what I consider the true or basic fact—that the heretical doctrines proclaimed were an epiphenomenon or rationalisation in terms of theological formulations masking—the *real* origin or first reality of the matter —an unconscious personality-situation of a definable type in the persons concerned. Here we leave the area of history pure and simple and enter the timeless area of human motive and motivation—failing understanding of which nevertheless historical events are but too apt to jig or jostle past our vision in tantalising meaningless succession, or worse still, merely to provide a number of coloured pieces which we subjectively fit together into a "historical" picture pleasing to prior preferential feeling.

I

It was grey day outside. In the chapter-house the light was little stained, lying in faint commingling shades across the flagged floor and over carved stone walls. The clergy in their black—in a row of stone seats at the end near the door giving access to the church—were almost natural-complexioned. But the Bishop's large face in the centre, still pallid from wounds received in a recent English invasion, appeared even more sickly because of the tinge thrown over it by his purple cassock and birettum. Shadowed pouches lay under his eyes: his air was weary and somewhat absent. He was reclining his bulky form sideways in his seat, an elbow resting on one stone arm while he tapped with his fingers on the other.

On his right hand, nearer the door into the church, a slender thin-nosed canon with an acid-precise expression was bending his head aside towards a red-faced, square built canon who sat next to him, whispering and nodding his head, holding some papers at which both were looking. On the Bishop's left hand an aged canon with silver hair, an air more dreamy and absent than the Bishop's own, sat looking straight in front of him with a gentle, rather senile smile on his almost too refined, aristocratic face. His abstraction and his slender height, the quiet hands folded before him, contrasted strongly with the air and person of the canon next on his left. This was a smallish, ruddy, fair-skinned man whose features and whole presence denoted alertness and a scarce-suppressed vivacity. With jet black hair and lively eyes, he seemed young to be a canon. He had just been speaking, making expressive movements of his hands, to the last canon in the row, on his left again, a rather pale-faced though robust looking man whose greying hair had not long since been fiery. He now turned his mobile dark eyes on the Bishop who at the same instant stirred, drew himself upright, and casting a glance about on either side, sighed. Looking across to someone beyond the open door he called out in a strong voice with a peremptory accent—"Let them come in!" He sighed again. A frown passed across his face.

They came in quietly and, at a sign from the Bishop, went and sat down on a form at some distance from the clerics, facing them. Two of them. One of the middle height, dark-haired, sallow and hollow-eyed, in the dress of a tradesman: the other a short, thick-set, broad-faced man wearing a soiled friar's habit, but with the friar's girdle of cord with its pendant knots signifying poverty, chastity and obedience replaced by a broad leather belt. The air of both was somewhat strange in the circumstances: they seemed in some way withdrawn, remote from their surroundings. The dark man in the tradesman's dress let his hollow eyes wander over the fretted walls and vaulted roof, though with no appearance of interest, and along the bench of ecclesiastics, but without seeming to take particular heed of them: the stout friar crossed one knee over the other and taking his chin in the stubby fingers of his hand—the beard he was growing was an inch long all round his face—rested his eyes on the ground as if meditating. There appeared to be nothing self-conscious or assumed in this —at any rate on the part of the tradesman. They seemed in some way actually "unreached" by their situation.

The clerics, on the other hand, were looking at them with interest, the Bishop leaning forward, narrowing his pouched eyes. Failing apparently to penetrate to their state, and coming back to the occasion, he sat up, coughed once behind his hand, and taking a paper which the acid-precise canon on his right held out to him, let his eyes travel over it. Then he raised his head and bending a severe look on the two men before him, pronounced:—

"Alexander Cock, baxter, and Robert Coltart, of the Order of the Friars Pauperites, ye are here compeared afore me and divers of the Chapter of this Diocese to be examinit anent certain heresies said to have been utterit and disseminated by you, and to thole the law an ye be guilty. Wherefore as the crime whereof ye are accused is capital, that is, of the heid, and accordant to the law of this Realm to be punishit with death, ye are bidden look weel unto yourselves and to answer in truth and verity all things charged against you, as men whase lives lie at the disposal of their judges."

The two were looking at him while he spoke, but still with some impersonality—they might scarcely have realised his purport.

"And firstly . . ." The Bishop lowered his eyes to the paper in his hands . . . "Firstly, Alexander Cock, these words:"—reading—"*God ordains some to everlasting life, others to everlasting punishment. God does not choose the Elect for ony guid He sees in them, or whilk he sees that they will do; nor does He select some for eternal reprobation because of their ill deeds foreseen by Him. It is impossible to assign ony reason for God's bestowing mercy on His people but just that it pleases Him: and neither has He ony reason for reprobating others but His will.*"

He sat frowning. "That's damnable doctrine!" he could be heard to say.

He raised his eyes—"Can ye truly hae said sic a thing, Cock?"

The dark man on whose face a smile of purest pleasure had appeared when he heard the doctrine read out by the Bishop, sprang up at once. In an instant extraordinarily changed. A flush suffused his brow; his sunken eyes shot fire.

"I said it!" he shouted in a defiant, exalted voice, "and the Word o' God said it afore me, and now *ye* hae said it, my lord Bishop, and blessed be God that I hae lived to hear a Prince of the Kingdom of Darkness proclaim the truth of God!"

He sat down. The friar beside him cried—"*Consentio!*" A silence fell.

"But, man, this . . . 'tis a grossness." It was the rumbling

77

bass of the square, red-faced canon nearest the door, on the Bishop's extreme right, protesting. He had heavy, overhanging eyebrows and looking forth under them rumbled: "An what ye say were true, Cock, it would mean that God has sent at ony rate *some* guid men to Hell and appointed some ill anes to Heaven. That maks God the doer of injustice—and that is impossible, since Justice is His Nature."

"Wha are ye . . ."—the baker was incensed again, and sprang up, pointing in accusation—"wha are *ye* that daurs limit God in His ain world? God is no to bind wi your *sequitoories* and your *sillyjimmies!* God's will is *free*,"—he threw his hands above his head—"free and abune aa!"

"*Nay!* Nay to that, Cock, as ye maintain it." The lively, young-looking canon had been restless in his seat, his eyes leaping from one person to another as they spoke in turn. Now he could no longer keep silent. "Ae thing God is no free to do," he cried over to the heretics, "and that is to deny His ain Nature. What is mair, could God do injustice here and now, Cock, ye would never ken it; for we and you and this braw kirk and the haill world and the universe entire would instantly dissolve into that naethingness out of the whilk God cried them into being. . . . For God created and sustains the universe by His Power, and God's Power *is* God's Justice. For God is Ane—*Ane*, mark that Cock!; ane absolutely single Being, indivisible, withouten pairts or accidents—His Power is His Justice and His Justice is His Truth and His Truth is His Luve and His Luve is His Power again, and sae through aa His attributes, as we presume to caa them; and ilk ane o these is God Himsel'; God's Justice is God Himsel', God's Power is God Himsel', and sae forrit. Because God is *Ane*." His tone and gestures were those of someone who would persuade another by patient exposition; the silver head of the canon by his side nodding the while affirmatively. "Therefore did He deny His Justice, whereby He rules creation, God would also by the same act and of necessity forswear His Power, whereby He made it and sustains it; with the instant consequent of universal dissolution and evanishment. And sae the solid world stands visible in your disproof, since it testifees against ye that God is still a God of Justice in that it witnesses that He is still a God of Power. And ye yoursel' refute your ain thesis in the act of stating it, since nane but a just

God could hae power to sustain ye in being, able to speak heresy. And sae ye see, Cock, that ye refute your doctrine in your ain person, for an what ye say were true ye couldna be here to say it, nor we to hear it."

The friar who had been smiling superiorly in his ball of beard, shrugged, smiling more widely. The baker after giving his attention for a while, knitting his brows as if trying to understand, had folded his arms and wrapped himself away. He now said nasally, swaying his head: "Think not to confound the Elect of God with philosophy and vain jangling."

The Bishop gave an impatient exclamation. "Ye're the ane to ken about jangling. I houp ye'll no come to ken about hanging."

"Wha is he that sall condemn?" the baker shouted in declamatory tones, springing up, *"It is Christ Jesus that died"*—he hesitated a moment in mid course as if taken aback, glancing in inquiry as all the clergy at the mention of the Divine Name uncovered their heads, then with an impatient shrug went on— *"Yea, that is risen also again, wha also maketh intercession for us!"*

Silence fell again.

"Nae doubt but ye can cite Scripture, Cock," said the Bishop at last. "But ye'll mind even Satan did that afore ye."

"Wha suld ken it better nor yoursel, my lord, since ye are his servant and he is your Maister."

The Bishop compressed his lips, reddening. "Cock," he said, controlling his voice. "I sair misdoubt ye for a contumacious heretic. Natheless I will condemn no man till it be certain he is no in error for want of hearing sound doctrine." He looked all about, saying aside: "Wha was deputit theologian?"

Ninian Kennedy had been seated by himself against the wall, on the side opposite the door, that is, to the Bishop's left, and between the clerics and the heretics. He got up and bowed, looking towards the Bishop. Just as he rose the sun came through the clouds, for suddenly like a silent acclamation the whole building floated warm with rainbow hues within, so that as the Bishop leant forward peering towards him crimson and purple changed across his face.

"Oh, it's you, is it, Ringean?"—sitting back again and looking forth at the heretics now stained in the multicoloured radiance

79

whether they would or not—"There's a mislearit knave here has said God decrees the eternal death of them that perish, and that no for ony ill that they may do. Let him hear true doctrine, if sae be he may retract his blasphemy." He clasped his hands above his stomach and with a wearied look prepared to listen.

Ninian Kennedy bowed. "My lord," he said in his mild voice, "it could easily be shown from mony texts of the Scriptures and the Fathers that God desireth the salvation of all that believe in Christ. As, however, the less is contained in the greater, it will suffice to show that God wills the salvation of all mankind whomsoever. Now St Paul saith in his Epistle to Timothy: *I desire therefore, first of all, that supplications, prayers, intercessions, and thanksgivings be made for all men. For this is guid and acceptable in the sight of God our Saviour, wha will have all men to be saved, and to come to the knowledge of the truth.*" He turned towards the heretics, saying: "The Apostle commandeth us to pray 'for all men' because this is 'guid and acceptable in the sight of God.' Wherefore is it guid and acceptable? Because 'God will have all men to be saved and to come to the knowledge of the truth.' In other words, God's will to save is universal." He turned towards the Bishop again: "The passage gangs on: *For there is ane God, and ane mediator of God and men, the man Christ Jesus*"—in a ripple of rising hands the clergy uncovered— "*wha gave Himself a ransom for all.*" Turning towards the heretics he repeated: "There is ane mediator of God and men, the man Christ Jesus. What doth this signifee? Plainly that the human nature which Christ assumed in the Incarnation is common to all men. Hence, wha ever is a man, has Christ for his mediator."

The heretics continued sitting side by side looking at him from the sides of their eyes. He therefore went on, speaking into the glowing building: "The Fathers and writers, my lord, are of ane accord in agreement. St Ambrose declares that God willeth to save all men: *He willed all to be His ain whom He establishit and creatit. O man, do not flee and hide thyself! He wants e'en those that flee, and doth not will that those in hiding suld perish.* St Gregory of Nazianzus haulds God's *voluntas salvifica* to be

80

co-extensive in scope with original sin and the atonement: *The law, the prophets, and the sufferings of Christ, by the whilk we were redeemed, are common property and admit of nane exception; but as all are participators in the same Adam, deceivit by the serpent, and subject to death per consequent of sin, sae by the heavenly Adam all are restorit to salvation and by the wood of ignominy recallit to the wood of life, from the whilk we had fallen.* St Prosper concludeth that, since all men are bounden in duty to pray for their fellow-men, God must needs be willing to save all without exception: *We maun sincerely believe that God willeth all men to be saved, since the Apostle solicitously prescribeth supplication to be made for all.* The question why mony perish St Prosper answers thus: *God willeth all to be saved and to come to the knowledge of the truth, therefore those that are saved, are saved because He wills them to be saved, while those that perish, perish because they deserve to perish."*

He sat down.

The Bishop was reclining in his chair, tapping the arms softly with his stout fingers, while he regarded the heretics shrewdly, his lips pouted and one eyebrow raised.

"Weel, Cock," he said, "that wad seem to answer ye. What will ye say now?"

The baker sprang up, instantly transfigured again.

"I say wi' the Word of God!" he shouted. Propelled by his energetic breath the rising motes went sailing through the colours in front of him and ascended towards the roof.

Raising his hand he shouted in a reciting voice: *"For this is the word of promise: At this time will I come, and Sara sall have a son. And not only she, but when Rebecca had conceived of our father Isaac"*—he pointed at Ninian Kennedy who had resumed his seat, but the pointing was quite impersonal: without knowing why Ninian Kennedy seemed at that moment to perceive something essentially simple and as it were personally inoffensive in the cast of the man's nature, along with whatever else was in it—*"For when the bairns were not yet born,"* he went on, *"nor had done ony guid or evil, that the purpose of God, according to election, might stand,"*—he jabbed into the air—*"not of works, but of him that calleth, it was said to her: The elder sall serve the younger. As it is written: Jacob have I luvit, but Esau have I hated."* He sat down, crossed his legs, threw his head on one side, and looked at Ninian Kennedy sideways under his lids.

"An it please you, my lord," said Ninian Kennedy rising, "this is from the ninth chapter of St Paul's Epistle to the Romans, whilk is the main reliance of them that hauld God absolutely predestinates some to guid and others to evil. The passage quoted is alleged to prove the absolute predestination of Jacob and the negative reprobation of Esau. But mony theologians have held that Esau was saved. And forbye"—he turned to the heretics— "the Apostle speaks not here of predestination to glory, but of Jacob's vocation to be the progenitor of the Messias. Esau, wha was not an Israelite but an Idumaean, was simply passit ower. The passage maun be interpret conform to the context, that is to say, as referring to the gratuity of grace, and nocht to pre· destination."

The baker had not altered his attitude as Ninian Kennedy proceeded, except after a little to take the end of his thin beard in the tips of his fingers and assume a mocking or superior expression. He got up. Extending his finger towards Ninian Kennedy unhurriedly, fixing him with his hollow glance, he recited: *"For He saith to Moses: I will have mercy on whom I will have mercy, and I will have compassion on whom I will have compassion"*— again he took fire— *"So then it is not of him that willeth, nor of him that runneth, but of God that showeth mercy. For the Scripture saith to Pharao: To this purpose have I raised thee, that I may shew my power in thee, and that my name may be declarit throughout all the earth."* He jabbed the air in rhythmic emphasis —*"Therefore he hath mercy on WHOM he WILL, and WHOM he WILL he HARDENETH!"* He sat down supremely satisfied and turning his head aside appeared to smile in his dark brown beard.

Ninian Kennedy rose. "My lord, the same may be said of this passage, which is from the same chapter. Some passages of the Scriptures would seem to imply that God withdraws His grace from them that are obdurate, nay, that He himself hardeneth their hearts in punishment of sin. Thus the Lord saith of Pharao in the Buik of the Exodus: *I sall harden his heart;* and Moses tells us: *The Lord hardened Pharao's heart, and he harkened not unto them.* But it would be wrang to assume that this denotes ane positive action on the part of God. Pharao, as we are tauld in the same Buik, *hardened his ain heart.* The faut in ilk' instance lies with the sinner, wha obstinately resists the call of grace. The Fathers speak of God's way of dealing with obdurate sinners in a manner whilk clearly shows their belief that He never entirely withdraws his mercy. They insist that the light of grace is never extinguishit in the present life. *God gave them ower to a reprobate mind,* says St Augustine, *for sic is the blindness of the mind. Whasoever is gien ower thereunto is shut out from the inward licht of God, but not wholly as yet, whilst he is in this life. For there is 'outer darkness,' whilk is understandit to belong rather to the day of judgment; that he suld rather be wholly without God, whosoever, whilst there is time, refuseth correction.*

"The theological argument, my lord, is weel stated by St Thomas. He distinguishes atween *obstinatio perfecta* and *obstinatio imperfecta* and saith: *Perfect obstinacy exists only in Hell. Imperfect obstinacy is that of a sinner wha has his will sae firmly set on evil that he is incapable of ony but the faintest impulses towards virtue, though e'en these are sufficient to prepare the way for grace.* Again, according to the declaration of the Fourth Lateran Council: *If ony faa into sin after having receivit Baptism, he can aye be restorit by sincere penance.*" He turned to the heretics. "Justly, therefore, does the Kirk regard despair of God's mercy as ane additional grievous sin. Whereas if they were richt wha assert that God in the end absolutely abandons the sinner, still mair that He predestines him to perish, there could be nane hope of forgiveness, and despair would be justifeed."

"O man, wha art thou that repliest against God?" The baker was up again, arms akimbo, his head held high. Now he had a prophetic or inspired air, as if he was merely a trumpet blown by some power that was not himself, potent though invisible . . . *"Wha art thou that repliest against God? Sall the thing formit say to him that formed it: Why hast thou made me thus? Or hath not the potter power ower the clay, of the same lump to mak ane vessel unto honour, another unto dishonour?"* He spread his hands on his buttocks and thrust his cheek forward—*"What if God, willant to shew his wrath, and to mak known his power, endurit with meikle patience vessels of wrath, fitted for destruction"*—standing erect and throwing out his chest—*"That he micht*

83

shew the riches of his glory on the vessels of mercy, whilk he hath preparit unto glory?"—throwing out his arms in a wide welcoming gesture and with head thrown back and half-closing eyes seeming to inhale deeply, the friar also beside him appearing to sniff the perfume—*"Even US . . . wham also he hath callit not only of the Jews, but also of the Gentiles."* He stood for a moment, then sat down and cast a challenging triumphant glance sideways at Ninian Kennedy.

The latter got up. "This is from the same chapter, my lord, and is their strongest text. Here the Apostle really seems to hae thought of predestination." (The friar: "Atweel does he!") "But the figure maun-na be pressed beyond what it will bear, lest we arrive at the heretical blasphemy that God positively predestined some men to heaven and others to hell. The *tertium comparationis* is nocht the act of the Divine Artificer, but the willantness of man to yield his will to God like clay in the hands of the potter." He turned to the heretics—"Nor is it admissable to read intil the Apostle's thought even a negative reprobation of certain men. For the primary intention of the Epistle to the Romans is to insist on the gratuity of man's vocation to Christianity and to reject the presumption that the Mosaic law and their bodily descent from Abraham gave the Jews preference ower the heathens. In short, the Epistle to the Romans has no bearing whatever on the speculative question whether or no the free vocation of grace is a necessary result of eternal predestination."

He was heard out impassively, the two looking from the sides of their eyes. But a flush could be seen deepening on the brow of the baker, his nostrils were twitching, and the priest had no sooner finished than he sprang up. . . .

"I am nocht hauden to the Romans, as ye appear to think. I stand upon the haill Word of God. Tak this out of the Ephesians —an ye hae read it ye will ken it again when ye hear it—*Accordant as he hath chosen us in Christ afore the foundation of the world. Wha hath predestined us unto the adoption of children through Jesus Christ"*—the clergy uncovered: the movement caught his eye and again he glanced aside at them impatiently—*"unto himsel, accordant to the purpose of his will. In whom also we are called by lot, being predestinated according to the purpose of him wha worketh all things accordant to the counsel of his ain will.* I am but an unlearit man, Messer Theologian, as my lord Bishop hath said, but to me 'all things' signifieth 'all things.' And so He also sends the damned to Hell, since He *'worketh all things accordant to the counsel of His ain will'."*

The friar rasped forth . . . *"Consentio."*

As Ninian Kennedy was rising the young-looking vivacious canon called out—"What saith the prophet Ezekiel? *As I live, saith the Lord, I desire not the death of the wicked, but that the wicked turn from his way and live. Turn ye, turn ye from your evil ways."*

The square red-faced canon on the Bishop's extreme right immediately rumbled, looking out from under his brows—"And doth not St Peter say in his Epistle: *The Lord delayeth not his promise, as some imagine, but dealeth patiently for your sake, not willant that ony suld perish, but that all suld return to penance."*

The Bishop nodded affirmatively then glanced over at the theologian, inviting him to continue.

Ninian Kennedy resumed: "An it please you, my lord, the passage cited proves nothing that is nocht a part of Christian doctrine. The Catholic Kirk has aye held that the saints are predestined. But equally it has aye condemnit the added doctrine of reprobation from eternity, whilk is heretical. As lang syne as the year of Our Lord, five-hunder and twenty-nine, at the Second Council of Orange, it was declarit: *We not only refuse to believe that some men are by divine power predestined to evil, but an if there be ony that hauld sic a wicked thing, we condemn them with utter detestation."*

"Amen," said the Bishop, "and rightly sae."

"This, my lord," the theologian continued, "is the doctrine of the heretic Calvin, and it is easily refuted baith from Revelation and from Tradition. As to Revelation, it runs counter to aa those mony texts of Scripture which assert the universality of God's saving will, the bestowal of sufficient grace upon all sinners, and the divine attribute of holiness. As to Tradition, the Fathers are of ane voice in upholding the orthodox teaching of the Kirk. The only ane wham the adherents of Predestinarianism hae daured to claim is St Augustine. Yet the Doctor of Grace expressly teaches: *God is guid, God is just. He can deliver some without merits*

85

*because He is guid; but he cannot damn ony without demerits,
because He is just.* St Prosper re-echoes this teaching when he
says of the reprobates: *Of their ain will gaed they out: of their
ain will they fell; and because their will was foreknown, they
were not predestined. They would, however, be predestined if they
were to return and persevere in holiness; hence God's predestination is for mony the cause of perseverance, for nane the cause of
falling away.* St Fulgentius also expresses himself in like
words. . . ."

"H'm, h'm!" . . . The acid precise canon sitting on the
Bishop's right hand broke in—"An it please you, my lord, the
baxter himsell stands in ane analogy! Your lordship sincerely
wills his liberation, but he will have nane of it, and sae, if he
persist, it micht be said he is nocht predestined to be set at liberty.
If, however, he acknowledge his error and cease from the propa-
gation of harmful doctrine, he would be liberated, and in that
case he would be predestined to liberation."

The Bishop inclined his head sideways but without taking his
eyes from the heretics . . . "Preceesely, Canon!" Raising his
hand he waved down what further Ninian Kennedy was about to
say and went on . . .

"Weel, Cock, your weary doctrine stands condemnit by the
Scriptures, and by the Fathers and the Tradition of the Kirk. And
lest there suld yet be doubt upon thee, I will now declare to thee
with authority, by virtue of mine office as ane bishop and pastor,
what is the mind of the Kirk in this matter. It is nocht given to
ony man to ken on earth what souls have gane or will gang to
perdition, but this we hauld siccarly, by the surety we possess of
God's honour and justice, that ilk ane lost is lost by his ain
choice; that the mercy of God is toward all His creatures, and
nane inherits the lot of the damned save him that casts awa God's
mercy, kennin fu' weel what it is he casts awa, and choosing to
be cut off from the light of God rather than forswear his sinful
will. Wha says contrariwise says heresy, and would imperil the
souls of Christians with despair, whereas hope is necessary for
salvation. Now, Cock, will ye receive the truth, or will ye persist
in error?"

The baker's brow was overcast with a hue of vexation, his
voice was angry—"Nae doubt but ye are heich, nae doubt but ye

86

are lifted up, that sit in pride and purple! But we have seen as heich and heicher evened with the lowermaist, when the arm of the Lord was suddenly streekit forth: and ye are but ane Herod for aa that, and the worms are ready that will devour ye!" He jumped up, thrusting out his chest, and shouted, with blazing eyes— "I will receive naething from thee, thou son of Belial, save submission to the Elect and their doctrine, whilk is God's doctrine! Yea, of a surety, do unto me what ye will that am led as a lamb to the slaughter, and like unto a sheep that is dumb afore her shearers, for I will not withhauld the testimony of my blude that it may rise up against you and your Chapter of idolators!" He seemed to become infuriated, shrieking—"And abune aa I will hear nae mair of your Fathers, nay, nor your mothers, not yet your sons and dochters! I will not admit even the angels of God that they suld judge my doctrine! But I will hae the Scriptures, and I will hae the Word of God, and *That* I will hae, and by that alane will I be judged!"

The friar cried again . . . *"Consentio!"*

The baker having sat down, noticing that some froth had fallen on his beard, swept it away with a casual downward motion of his open hand.

II

The canon with the silver hair, on the Bishop's left, still smiling his old-man's smile, made a tut-tutting sound with his tongue, and with his eyes closed, shook his head slowly from side to side. The young looking, ruddy canon beside him gave a shrug and a grimace, and looked at his neighbour on the left, who avoided his glance, stroking his forehead with his fingertips. The acid-precise canon on the Bishop's right was looking on the floor, drawing his fingers with a pulling motion down the ridge of his thin nose: while the square red-faced canon beside him, who had the look of a certain kind of very straightforward, unsubtle man, was simply staring out under his overhanging eyebrows. The Bishop was compressing his lips, and seemed in some doubt, or swither of impulse or intention, with regard to the heretics, studying meanwhile the causes of his offence. Ninian Kennedy was also studying them, with his mild, open glance: already that curious air, of remoteness, or insensibility of their predicament, had returned upon them. The baker appeared to be making some sort of chewing movements with his mouth, his eyes travelling emptily around over the stained stonework of floor and fretted walls.

The Bishop seized his course, having to get on with it, picked up the paper from where it had been lying on his knees, and clearing his throat twice loudly, so that the sound re-echoed, read out in his former judicial tone, but this time frowning—

"Secondly, Alexander Cock, these words: *Neither contrition, nor penance, nor ony other virtue, but faith alane is the medium or instrument by the whilk we are justifeed, and apprehend the grace of God, the merits of Christ and the remission of sins; guid works in particular are nocht but filthy clouts, righteousnesses of Pharisees and derogatory to the merits of Christ."*

"Did ye say that, Cock?"

"I baith said it and will say it again."

The friar . . . *"Et ego consentio!"*

The Bishop moved his eyes round to Ninian Kennedy. "He'll no tak the Scriptures *and* the Fathers: e'en gie him the Scriptures *without* the Fathers."

Ninian Kennedy rose . . . "My lord . . . The teaching of the Scriptures in regard to the pairts played by faith and guid works in the process of justification may be summarised thus: first, a man may believe ilk' article of our religion and yet be lost for want of guid works or because he hath not the love of God. Consequently, faith alane does not justifee nor insure eternal salvation. Our Divine Saviour Himself declares: *Not everyone that saith to me, Lord, Lord, sall enter into the kingdom of heaven, but he that doeth the will of my Father who is in heaven, he sall enter into the kingdom of heaven.* St James saith: *Do ye not see that by works a man is justifeed, and not by faith alane?* And St Paul: *If I suld have all faith, so that I could remove mountains, and have not charity, I am nothing . . .* Second, forbye faith, justification requires certain other preparatory or dispositive acts. There is, for example, the fear of divine justice; as it saith in Ecclesiasticus: *He that is without fear can nocht be justifeed.* Also, hope in God's mercy; as in Romans: *For we are saved by hope.* Again, charity; as in Luke: *Mony sins are forgiven her*

88

because she hath luvit much. Furthermore, contrition or penitence; as in Luke again: *Unless ye sall do penance, ye sall all likewise perish.* Finally, guid works in general; as in St James: *So faith also, if it have not works, is dead in itself."* He turned and faced the heretics, and said in a reasonable tone—"Nane that ponders these and other sic texts can maintain, as do Calvin and others, that the guid works mentioned merely accompany justification, for they are unmistakably describit as causes whilk dispose and prepare the sinner for it." He faced back to the Bishop—"Third, it is nocht faith alane that justifees, but faith informit and actuated by charity. As it saith in Galatians: *For in Christ Jesus neither circumcision availeth onything, nor uncircumcision; but faith that worketh by charity.* The Greek text, my lord, shows that the word *operatur* in the Vulgate maun be ta'en passively, so that a mair correct version of the same wad be 'but faith effected or formit by charity'. But the meaning is in substance the same, that is, a deid faith, withouten charity, availeth nothing. As St James saith: *For even as the body wanting the spirit is deid, so also faith without works is deid.* And soothly, my Lord, the Epistle of St James might be ta'en throughout as ane refutation in general of the doctrine of justification by faith without works."

The baker gave a superior shrug and ejaculated—"James is ane Epistle of Strae!"

"Now he'll no hae the Apostles!" remarked the young-looking ruddy canon aside.

The baker heard: he sprang up—"I will hae ane Apostle! And I will hae Paul when he says in the Romans: *For we account a man to be justifeed by faith alane—without the works of the Law!"*

The Bishop sat forward—"What's that? 'Faith alane'? Do I gang to schule to the heretics?"

The young-looking ruddy canon was laughing silently. Ninian Kennedy himself smiled. He said: "The word 'alane' does not occur in the texts, my lord. It was inserted by the heretic Luther, wha sought thereby to establish his doctrine by deceiving the ignorant, and is ane of the alterations or glosses in those heretical Scriptures whase reading in consequent is forbidden the laity. The context shows that it is a falsification. The Apostle contrasts justifying faith, not with those acts preparatory of salvation which spring from it, but with the barren 'works of the law', that is, of the Auld Testament, which, as sic, possessed nae mair power to justifee than the guid works of the heathen. This was pointed out lang syne by St Augustine, whom I cite not as a Father, but because he states the question mair clearly than it is my puir talent to do. 'Unintelligent persons,' quoth St Augustine, 'with regard to the Apostle's statement: *We conclude that a man is justifeed by faith without the works of the Law,'* have thocht him to mean that faith is sufficient for a man, even if he leads a bad life and has no guid deeds to allege. It is impossible that sic a character suld be deemed 'a vessel of election' by the Apostle, wha, after declaring that 'in Christ neither circumcision availeth onything nor uncircumcision,' adds the important remark 'but faith that worketh by charity,' It is sic faith that separates the faithful children of God from unclean devils—for even these 'believe and tremble', as the Apostle James saith, but they do no guid works. Therefore they possess not the faith by the whilk the just man lives—the faith which operates through love in sic wise that God recompenses it accordant till its works with eternal life'. Thus St Augustine."

He was proceeding, but the Bishop, who had begun to look fatigued, held up his hand.

"See where ye stand now, Cock," he said. "Ye hae putten forrit twa propositions—the first, that the Scriptures are the sole authority for Christians; the second, that justification is by faith alane, without charity and guid works. And the tane o' your propositions has killed the tither. Whilk of the twa will ye now renounce, therefore; for since justification by faith alane is condemnit by the Scriptures, ye maun either now gie up the Scriptures as your authority or else forswear your doctrine of salvation by faith alane."

The thin voice of the canon with the silver hair broke in. " 'Tis dangerous, 'tis very dangerous!"

All looked at him.

He was looking straight before him dreamily, and appeared to be reflecting aloud . . . "Wha then will avoid sin or work guid till his neighbour? They say the heretiics say: *Pecca fortiter et crede firmius!"** He relapsed into silence, shaking his head.

* Sin strongly and believe the more firmly—LUTHER.

The square red-faced canon rumbled in his bass—"But, my lord, but this is a new thing, and nocht faith! Faith—the faith necessary for salvation—has aye been understandit as ane act of the intellect, assenting to the truths revealed by God. The heretics would even it with *fiducia*, whilk is not faith but *trust* or *confidence*—ane act of the will therefore, not of the intellect!"

"Aye, that is it!" exclaimed Ninian Kennedy involuntarily, recognising what he had himself been about to say. The Bishop glanced at him, then back at the heretics.

"Weil, Cock!" he said. "I await your answer!"

"I will answer ye!" said the baker getting up, flushed as it seemed for the moment even more with vexation than with anger. "And I will ask you, where gat *ye* the spirit of interpretation that ye suld declare unto *me* the interpretation of Haly Writ?"

The young-looking vivacious canon snorted and sat forward— "Where gat *ye* that spirit, that ye suld declare it unto *us*?"

The baker had barely reached his seat: he straightened again —"Wha but the sancts of God, suld hae the power to interpret the Word of God!"

"Are ye then sancts already?"

The baker set his shoulders and with head held back glanced down along his nose—"Thou hast said it!"

The square canon rumbled, "Show us your surety!"

The baker lifted up his eyes on him. *"The Spirit itself beareth witness with our spirit that we are the children of God,"* he quoted. "And by that Spirit do we declare and make known the Truth unto you that are hauden in darkness, if sae be your darkness may be lichted up by the licht that is in huz!"

The Bishop snorted in turn. "Man, Cock! ye pass aa! *We* interpret Scripture by nane inward and private, and therefore uncertain illumination; but openly, by the light of Reason, and conform to the harmony of doctrine in its divers parts, and under the authority of the Kirk. (And, mark you, Cock, the Kirk has the richt to interpret Scripture, for it is the Kirk that guarantees the authority of Scripture, which indeed was first written in proof and witness of the doctrines of the Kirk.) But ye, Cock, in despite of Reason, wad mak the Scriptures witness till their ain authority —Nothing, nor no man, Cock, can witness till his ain authority; but all authority, save only God, is witnessed till from without

91

and from above—(it is not what *I* say—as if *I* were somebody—but what I say that is accordant to Reason, or what I say by virtue of the authority gi'en me by another, whase authority, in turn, is establishit.) But ye, Cock, when bidden show your title to interpret Scripture, point—not to that without, that might guarantee it—but to your ain breist—as if there was ocht in there but wind and your mislearit heart! My word upon it, Cock, ye weary me! Argue your case nor prove yoursel' ye cannot; ye but assert and play the oracle. And your emptiness of sound reason ye are fain to cloak with a windy sough of words!"

The baker had risen. He was crimson. Pushing backwards the fists he held clenched by his sides and bending himself forward, he shouted, shaking his beard at the clerics—"Stuffed cassocks! Whited walls! Speak ye to me of Reason! What, i' faith, is Reason?"—with hands and eyes seeking an answer from the surrounding air—"Reason is a whure! Reason is the Devil's greatest whure!"*—setting his arms akimbo and advancing his side-face—"Does the Reason gie licht? Aye, verily, like the licht dung would gie forth were it putten in a lanthorn!"

He stopped abruptly, opening his eyes wide. His mouth fell open. A smile had appeared on every face! The young ruddy-faced canon was laughing outright and without disguise, throwing back his head. The silver-haired canon wore a bland smile on his blind-looking upturned face, while the robust recently fiery-haired canon at the end of the row put up his hand along his brow to screen his features while his shoulders trembled. The acid precise canon had again taken his thin nose in his finger-tips, and was looking at the ground aside, his cheeks filling spasmodically behind his close-pressed lips. Even the Bishop allowed himself a small smile that turned down the corners of his mouth.

The heavy, somewhat puzzled look had lifted for the first time from the square canon's red face at the end of the row nearest the door. His nostrils twitched and his eyes twinkled under their overhanging brows as he rumbled—

"How cam ye to that about the Reason, Cock? By the use of reason, or without? If by reason your judgment maun be fause, since accordant to your ain sell ye have won till't by the use of ane incapable instrument—the Reason. Your statement—do

* Luther.

92

ye no see?—contradicts itsel, since ere it could be true the
Reason would need to gie ye licht eneugh at least to show ye it
gies nane . . . Or do ye admit that without reason ye hae con-
demned the Reason?"

The ruddy young-looking canon laughed—"Nae reasonable
road from Reason, Cock. 'Tis what ye ca' a *sequitoorie*."

The baker, with an eagle eye glancing from one to the other,
tightly pursing his lips, was suddenly shaken like a wisp.

"Lauch! Lauch, sons of Belial," he shrieked, while the beard
trembled on his quaking jaw—"Lauch, children of perdition!
Whuremongers! Idolators! Unclean! Lauch, ye limbs of Satan!
worshippers of the Abomination! Bloody persecutors! Aye,
lauch—but the day cometh, and is now come, when He that sitteth
in the heavens sall lauch! Yea, verily, the judgment is e'en now
without the door! Ye will be bound thegether like faggots to be
cast intil the furnace of the wrath of God"—his fervish, sunken
eyes fixing upon the Bishop—"Aye, and you also, my lord Bishop,
even you, together with your lordship's bastards and their dam
the painted Jezebel that lay in your lordship's bed!"

III

The Bishop's cheeks trembled, turning purple. *"A veechk!*
. . ."* he spat forth, then cut the words off at the lips and sat
lowering. Something passing across his face seemed to wipe the
features to a hardness as of rock. His eyes had become small and
hard above their pouches.

"Cock," he said at last impressively in a voice that trembled,
"I give you my word that when first I heard your doctrines it gaed
across my mind that you maun be in jest, though the jest, i' faith,
was ill chosen. I ken now it was nae jesting with you—and pity
it is, and pity for all your crew, for could ye jest ye wad ne'er
wander sae far from all reason and guid sense. Natheless
although ye cannot jest I trow ye be ower light-minded. Here
ye stand—chargit with a crime that by the law of this realm is
to be punishit with death. So ye might truly be said here to stand
in the ante-chamber of the Judgment. An ye prove-na mair tract-
able ye may stand afore your Maker—aye, ere twa suns have set

—to thole His dread assize and answer for the haill sins committed in your life. Yet sae light-minded are ye, ye bear yoursell as gin ye were but flyting in the mercat-place, and your meat waited ye on the buird at your ain fireside. First ye put forrit doctrines baith absurd and damnable; syne when it is faithfully shown ye they are no maintainable, instead of retracting them as would a guid-willant reasonable man, ye change about to hurling accusations on the ground of morals—(*He that is without sin, let him first cast the stane!*) Twa things suld be evident, even till an unlearit man, for sic ye truly say ye are: the first, that the truth and salutary nature of sound doctrine are nocht impugnit by the moral state of its defenders and representatives; the second, that when ye come to answer for your ain sins it will nocht avail ye to cite the douncomings of others, though they were those of a bishop. Standing as ye are on the doorstane of the Judgment it behoves ye weel to accuse yoursell afore your ain conscience, if sae be it will stead ye better when ye face your reckoning. Yet of this ye show nae sense, as if ye had nocht to answer for; or,—what seems mair likely—as if your inward state was the maist real and present thing with ye, and dulled perception of the position in the whilk ye stand.

"Cock, I look at ye and I wonder. What is it that ails ye? Did ye in truth seek pure doctrine, and that out of a pure heart and unfeignit mind, ye would embrace it gladly. But you when ye are gien pure doctrine will no receive it—nay, but haud the mair to that whilk is fause. So then I perceive it is not pure doctrine that ye crave, and for the sake of pure doctrine—ye hae deceived us there, and wad deceive others, making a profession—but what ye seek is something other, something that ye hope to gain *by means of fause doctrine.* If sae, we but waste wind upon ye, for your heresy lies not within the mind, but abides in some distemper of your will, in your desires and your affections.

"Cock, I hae dealt fairly by ye. I will do fairer yet. I will say in charity that ye may be a pure soul, and that ye may have been offended at the conduct of some. So far as I am accused in person ye do me less than justice. It is true that when a youth, and afore ever I was a priest, I was handfasted, and of that union had issue like another. If it was a sin in me, though sanctioned by the custom of the realm, I was guilty of it; and I sall answer for it afore Him Wha will yet judge me and all men. But of other sin of like carnal nature afore God I declare me innocent. But there are others—aye, shame that I suld say it, even in this diocese!—whase conversation has been neither lawful nor circumspect, unworthy pastors of God's flock, whase courses have offendit 'little anes' of tender conscience—sic like, it might be, as yoursell . . .

"Cock, I will mak a bargain with ye. Your doctrines are damnable, for they impugn the chiefest tenet of our holy religion, the love of God and His saving will towards all our sinful human kind. And they will be interpret by mony in the sense that guid works are of nane account, and so against law and conscience they will fall in sins for which, repenting not, they may be damned. Ye will see that ye canna be looten lowse to sow despair of God's mercy among puir souls that we haud it in commission to protect against pernicious error; and to gie cause to some whereby they will damn their sowls. For to spread heresy, Cock, besides a crime afore the law, is the greatest of aa the sins against our neighbour, since it consists in perilling his chances of eternal blessedness. Sae I will strike ane compact with ye . . . They say ye mak guid breid . . . Gie me your solemn word to keep your notions to yoursel' in your ain bakehoose till ye come to see mair reason. And for my part—though some clergy be bad, yet there be mony guid—gie me your word to quell your tongue, and I will gie ye *my* word, that as it hath been my labour heretofore, sae and even mair sall it be my labour henceforward, that the guid will be suffered and the evil sall be reformed, an I brook life!"

The baker got up. He started calmly . . . "I will make nane bond with the mammon of iniquity"—but immediately blazed up, holding his face sideways and throwing forward a threatening and accusing forefinger—"nay, nor with thee, thou braying ass! And the mair as, though ye ken it not, it rests not in your hands to fill ane compact. Life does not remain to ye to reform ocht. For the judgment against idolators has gane forth, the writing is on the wall against ye! Woe to thee, thou bloody man, when the suffering sancts of God put their hands to the work, and the judgment of the Righteous sall be executed upon thy body!"

The Bishop, having leant back in his seat, moved his hand and said wearily: "If I be even as you say, ane ass, and if ye be a prophet as ye appear to think, let me remind you there was a time already when *a dumb ass, speaking with man's voice, rebuked the madness of a prophet.*" He roused himself and sat forward—"And if they be threats against me that ye have uttered, I am nothing dauntened, though some among ye be men of blude that work by stealth. I did not put on this purple for a decoration to my person, I have wrocht a lang day in the vineyard—let my deeds testifee!—and if impious men, traitors to God and their country, would tak awa my life, I will round it out like ane true Scot and ane leal son of Holy Kirk—and I will have this purple for my shroud!"

He sat back . . . "However, Cock, that day is na yet, and I am nocht here to be judged by you, but ye are here to be judged by me."

He took up from his knee the bill of indictments as if to read the next in order of the heretical propositions. But groaned . . .

"Och! there's a great mony things here yet!"—and lowered it, saying, "What boots it? Enow is enow!"

Holding the paper straight out towards the heretics and assuming a judicial voice, he said: "Alexander Cock! Ye have uttered heresy in the hearing of all present, and I solemnly charge thee now, wilt thou recant these propositions, keeping weel in mind, if no, that under the law of this realm the crime is punishable with death." He added, "An ye will crave time . . ."

The baker stood up.

"I want nane," he said without excitement, and indeed a kind of pride and dignity. "Neither for thee nor for all the devils in Hell, will I recant ane word of what *ye* call heresy, but what *I* call Christ's Evangel, the message of saving grace poured out upon us wha are God's Elect, chosen in Him afore the beginning of the world!"

"It sufficeth!"

The Bishop opened his hand. The Paper of the indictment, after two fluttering swoops this way and that, skimmed sailingly away above the floor and fell lightly to rest not far in front of the heretics' feet.

The Bishop rose up, very solemnly. "Alexander Cock! I pronounce you guilty of heresy, I can do no other . . ."

A shout from the baker went up . . . "The water, my lord! Ye forget the water!"

The Bishop stopped. Everyone looked with surprise at the baker, who sat, still wearing his air of pride and dignity, his head held high.

"Aye!" said he, folding his arms and with head slightly aside glancing at the wall—"Bid them bring in the water!"—with an ironical twist of his mouth—"This is the place! . . . 'Tis in the play!"

All around the expressions relaxed in understanding, with glances of reproof or scorn. The Bishop said testily—"I am nae mair Pilate than ye are Christ; ye speak blasphemously in imputing it to yoursell . . ." Reassuming his judicial tone, he said . . . "I pronounce you, Alexander Cock, guilty of heresy, and I now relax you to the secular, to be ta'en back from whence ye came and there to underlie the law!"

The baker, seated in his place, raised a harsh exultant shout. "Yea, of a surety, truly is it written: *For thy sake we are putten to death aa the day lang. We are accounted as sheep for the slaughter.*"

The Bishop raised his hand palm outward before his face, turning his head away—"Cock, ye deave me!"

But then he turned back, and stood, with a penetrating and discerning look fixed on the baker . . .

"Ye hae rejected the Kirk, and the Fathers, and the faculty of Reason, and the Scriptures unless ye be looten wrest them as it suits ye—rejected, in guid sooth, aathing except Cock!"

He paused, narrowing his eyes. His hands clenched themselves.

With head and shoulders thrust forward in the direction of the baker—"Cock!" he said, with an accent of intensity, "I ken ye now! . . . Ye are aa cocks thegether—*and ye wad mak a dungheap o' Scotland so that ye might craw on the tap o't!*"

He turned to go. The canons had also risen; their unequal height was seen. The acid-precise canon in the Bishop's path said: "H'm, h'm, my lord, what of the friar Coltart? Will ye examine him, or as he has subscribit the heresies of the other sall he also be adjudged guilty?"

The Bishop stopped, and turning again bulkily, fixed a long, heavy look on the friar, expression draining from his eyes. And pronounced . . . *"Consentio!"*

The friar had throughout given the impression of trying to thrust himself forward into the proceedings, by way of his un-asked-for comments and a certain something forced and exaggerated in his postures and facial expressions of indifference or disdain. Now he leapt up as if stung. They heard him catch his breath. His inch-long beard bristled, his blue eyes paling in his flaming face. Casting a venomous, reproachful, hurt, offended look at the Bishop, he scraped his foot across the floor.

VI

With this I hope we have taken a great step towards an understanding of our subject.

We have in the first place learned what the principal Reformation doctrines were—and a great surprise it will have been to most of us who now call ourselves Protestants: many will have heard them with horror. (Although in fact it is still not so very long ago —I am speaking of lifetimes—since it could be heard said of a minister, with critical scorn, "He preached an ethical sermon," meaning in effect that he had urged on his congregation the merit of acting well, on the Calvinistically illicit assumption that good works were in fact really good and possible, whereas according to sound Reformation doctrine they were neither, and were in addition irrelevant to the great question of the individual's election and salvation). We shall have seen too that the Reformers could not in free debate hold their own even on their own chosen ground of Scripture; that in fact the Reformation doctrines were not found in Scripture at all—except insofar as they were put there by those who "found" them.

And this led us on to the really momentous but inescapable discovery, which began in the end to dawn as a suspicion on the Bishop, that the *real* cause of the Reformers' heresy was not to be looked for in erors of judgment on doctrine or in the intellect at all, but in a deviation of the *will;* that they were not in reality seeking the truth of doctrine but were in fact seeking some doctrine —any doctrine—which could be held and advanced in justification of an event in their inner world, a movement of their will, *which had already taken place, i.e. prior to the presence of the doctrine in their mind.* It should be printed in leaded type, for it is the crux, that *the conflict about doctrine was a shadow show.* The real event—assuming the good faith of the heretics on trial, which must always be assumed—was under the conscious; but as they were sixteenth century men the explanation of their inner state when they perceived one or when one arrived to them or dawned upon them was bound to be in terms of theological propositions, because it was a theologically preoccupied century and a—in modern parlance—"rationalisation" in other than

99

theological terms would in those days have been incomprehensible and would not have made their position "clear" either to their contemporaries or to themselves.

The next following chapter in the book was designed to illustrate just how the subconscious inward state in a particular individual preceded in terms of causation the conscious act of perceiving the "truth" of Reformation doctrines, how the truth of the doctrines was "perceived" not because they were objectively "there" but because they expressed, explained and justified a condition already present in the subject—in this case, of course, our main protagonist, the priest who was to become a Reformer, John Tod. (What had to be done in this giving an account of John Tod's "conversion" was something exceedingly difficult; for one had to *convey*—not describe—to the reader a clear view of events in a clouded and tumultuous consciousness without by a word suggesting there was any conscious clearness of the event where the sufferer himself was concerned. That is, one had to find a way to convey *only* what he himself was conscious of in obscure and distressful fashion, but yet do it in such a way as to convey also, and clearly—to the reader, that is—what he was *not* conscious of and could not penetrate to, that is, the primary causation in the personality of his condition, the reasons below consciousness of his state, what was *really* happening in him. In such a case we must not on any account, if the rules of art are to be observed, wade into the subject's consciousness as if it were a den of cats in conflict and pick up one animal after another in order to call the reader's or spectator's attention to its "points").

What had happened was that John Tod still in fear and horror of heretics and ignorance of their doctrines—(we must recall here that to anyone of that time who was not of their number Protestants were still a tiny and vociferous group of revolutionaries of some kind or other who propounded some sort of absurd doctrines, destroyed public buildings, and were suspected of being, if not known to be, in treasonable league and correspondence with the English)—John Tod having gone in fear and anger to witness the event, with a tumultuous confusion of horror and astonishment, eagerness and shrinking, *recognised his own spirit in action*

100

in the heretics at what was to have been their hanging (they were in fact rescued and carried off at the last minute by the local "hyena," a lordling called Pitfourie, as had been arranged from the outset). Not, as he now realised, having known himself what he expected, he had in fact seen the heretics exalted, beatified, never ceasing to apostrophise the assemblage that packed the square and crowded the forestairs and windows, calling down threats and maledictions on their derision, shouting with unabated testimony; while as they spoke all the high things of the world came tumbling down, and every topmost stone was laid lower than the lowermost, the mighty of the land left their places, the exalted were abased, mitred heads rolled in the dust, and the mouths were stopped of those that sat above and taught the people. And taking scope through that universal downfall—that *douncome*—the doctrine of the pure Word filled the land, and the Elect, its oracles, mounted to the places left vacant by the fallen mighty. . . . Meanwhile a flush glorified their brows, and over their heads, and on their behalf, there was not the gallows, but a blowing of trumpets, a breaking of seals, and the pouring forth of the vials of the wrath of God upon their persecutors. . . .

He came away shaken by an appalling inward tumult—*because knowing somehow deep-inwardly that he had seen himself.*

Obviously there remained for him but to encounter the doctrines which justified such a movement of the spirit as theirs and his, and whose "truth" he would in consequence immediately perceive, so that he also might become a stander above the mighty and the multitude and his voice too—and even more than Cock's —might fill the land.

101

VII

"In the name of the Father, and of the Son, and of the Holy Ghost. . . .

"Brethren. . . ."

Ninian Kennedy is in the pulpit. He has mounted there to speak with the hope of counteracting a tendency to panic in the people, for the Protestants in the form of a mob from a neighbouring town led by Pitfourie are known to be in the vicinity and the church is threatened, while at the same time from an accustomed reflex a great number have taken refuge in it.

He is speaking about heresy, and with this we ought, we feel —it is high time—to be approaching the forecourt of the arcane regions of the ultimate causation of the Reformation.

He begins by laying the foundation, that is, by establishing the Church's right and duty to be the teacher of all men at all times in all matters concerning faith and morals.

"When Our Lord Jesus Christ at the first, before His Ascension into Heaven, laid upon the Apostles their mission to the world, the words that He used were these: *All power is given to me in heaven and in earth. Going therefore teach ye all nations, baptising them in the name of the Father, and of the Son, and of the Holy Ghost. Teaching them that they should observe all things whatsoever I have commanded you. And behold I am with you all days, even to the consummation of the world.*"

Note again that I am writing throughout not as a Catholic protagonist or any kind of protagonist, but as an historian. That is to say my objective is not to impose any *view* on the past but to find out and illuminate *what was there*. I am not here arguing for the authenticity of the mandate of the Catholic Church but endeavouring to show in what light that mandate and commission was seen by Christians for fifteen hundred years before the Reformation, as by Catholics since. If you are a historian and you have to write about Catholics you write about them as they actually were and according to what they actually believed; you do not, ignoring that, tell them what in your opinion they *ought* to have believed, either now or all those years ago. So very many who regard themselves as historians do little in effect but hector and upbraid the persons of the past for having been men of their time—this from the supposedly high superior altitude of a contemporary rostrum, all our modern notions and superstitions taken for granted as the ultimate, final truth against which everything else or everything previous has to be tested.

Here then was the warrant and commission of the Apostles and their successors the pastors of Christ's Church right up to the present and in all times coming. "Jesus Christ receivit from His Father *all power in heaven and in earth*: and per virtue of this power *He* sends *them—even as His Father sent Him—to teach* not one but *all nations*, and instruct them in *all truths*. And that He may assist them effectually in the execution of this His commission, He promised to be with tñem, not alone for the lifetime of the Apostles, not alone for three, or four, or ten generations, but *all days, even to the consummation of the world*."

There then was the Christian Church's commission, laid upon it by God in the person of His Son, "and joinit thereto God's promise, whereby all men in all times may be assured that that which the Kirk teaches is the truth. And woe be unto us, brethren, woe be unto us if we do not God's bidding and proclaim not unto all men in all times all those truths that were given unto us and were to be for the salvation of the world."

But—"if it be the Kirk's mission to proclaim and teach the truth, it must follow as a part of that same that it is Her duty to *protect* the truth which She proclaims, and preserve it from the errors to which the mind of man is in all ages and conditions prone. And so it is that in every age a part of the Kirk's activity, in the execution of Her commission, which She has from God, has aye had to be the combating of heresy."

Already Ninian Kennedy has touched upon a point which it is essential to grasp from the outset if the Reformation movement is to be seen in focus—and which in fact never was grasped by us as we grew up into the Evangelical Faith, any more than it was apprehended by our mentors, or for that matter understood by the Reformers themselves. We have always been accustomed to think, and still think (whatever our attitude to it) of the Reformation as a unique event in history, the product of a new or fresh "perception," a unique "next step" in the "progress" of things— whereas in fact heresy, *and heresy of the same essential type as*

103

that which triumphed at the Reformation, had been an active element in and a feature of practically every age since the Church began. It only triumphed in certain areas—most completely in Scotland—in the sixteenth century because strong political and economic elements happened to be also active in the field, and allied themselves with it. At all other times it had been suppressed—otherwise, let it be realised, there would have been no civilisation called Europe; we should not have had our European heritage. There are those among us today who "couldn't care less" about European civilisation and who are in the strict sense of the term, that is, in that they are separated from their natural traditions, barbarians; but there are still those who do care about the great European tradition and those ought to realise that its development depended throughout upon the suppression of interior elements hostile to it, that would have destroyed it.

In effect, heresy was so much not a unique feature of the sixteenth century that one would be justified in calling it an element in human nature at all times. We have been quite wrong in thinking of the Reformation as something whose nature it was to succeed. Its success was accidental and "of the time"; its nature was—and is—always there. What is it?

Ninian Kennedy first defines a heretic as, in the Greek from which the word comes, "one who picks and chooses"; in matters of faith it means one who chooses out for himself doctrines which he will believe, rejecting others. And as there are almost as many opinions as there are men, so there are almost as many heresies as there are heretics. Heresy is therefore at first sight a very difficult thing to bring to judgment before the mind as a thing *in itself,* since to define it it will not suffice merely to enumerate its various forms; that would be to substitute description for definition. "As therefore it would be thankless, as endless, to seek for the essence of heresy in the variety of its actual forms, let us rather see if there be not in all forms some constant or common element; if so be that by consideration of what they have in common we may win to an understanding of the nature of the thing itself. For if there be that which heresy is *in itself,* it will manifestly be revealed in that respect in which all heresies agree, rather than in those many in which they differ."

He is immediately reminded of two points on which however else they differ all heretics are agreed, "and these two things are, first, in that they deny that God our Lord is Really Present in the Sacrament of the Altar, and second, in refusing with an equal violence to honour her who was the Mother of Christ, God the Son, come on earth in the form of Man." And he asks: "Can that universal agreement of heretics on these two heads tell us anything of the inward nature and essence of heresy?"

Here again I pause to insist that it is no part of my purpose to argue for the truth of the doctrine of the Real Presence or the appropriateness of honour to be paid to the Virgin Mary. That is so far away from my intention that in fact my purpose would be unaffected even were the Christian religion proved to be false or no more than a collection of fables and superstitions. We who grew up as Protestants know the attitude we were brought up to, "conditioned" to if you will, in each of those matters and to us it seems but natural that anyone should reject both. The point is that here we are dealing with men, the Reformers, who were brought up, "conditioned," both to believe in the doctrine of the Real Presence and to honour the Virgin Mary, both of which were attitudes of mind which had been for fifteen hundred years universal in their society. Why did *they* break with their conditioning in those two respects and precisely in those two respects?

We may approach the point by means of the actual words of Ninian Kennedy's sermon. He said: "As to the first, there has never been a time when the Kirk has not held and taught that Christ is Truly and Really Present in this Blessed Sacrament— and I may remind ye again of Christ's promise to preserve His Kirk from error. But I pass that by, because, as we weil ken, the heretics will not receive the authority of the Kirk. Again, there is the experience of us whose souls have ere now been wounded unto life in the Communion of this Sacrament, whereby our being has been filled with His light. But that also I pass by, for we ken also that no heretic will abide the judgment or regard the experience of another. But they claim to accept the Scripture, and the judgment of the Scripture they maun therefore abide whether they will or no.

"What then saith the Scripture? In the Holy Gospel of Sanct John we read these words: I am the living breid which came doun

105

from heaven. If ony man eat of this breid, he sall live forever; *and the breid that I will give is my flesh, for the life of the world.* The Jews therefore strove among themselves, saying: How can this man give us his flesh to eat? Then Jesus said to them: Amen, amen, I say to you: *Except ye eat the flesh of the Son of man, and drink his blude, ye sall not have life in you. He that eateth my flesh, and drinketh my blude, hath everlasting life; and I will raise him up in the last day. For my flesh is meat indeed, and my blude is drink indeed. He that eateth my flesh, and drinketh my blude, abideth in me, and I in him. As the living Father hath sent me, and I live by the Father; sae also he that eateth me, the same also sall live by me."*

He paused and with an effect of extraordinary emphasis said quietly . . .

"My dear brethren, He that spake these words was God. He baith said He was God and proved it by His mony miracles, chief of aa by His rising from the tomb. If these words be not true, God is a liar, and the haill body of Christians from that day till this, have lived and died in error. deceived by their Creator. Nor will it avail to say, as the heretics do, that He spake but in a figure. For if it was sae then in a figure He deceivit His Apostles, and the Kirk that He founded through them was founded by Him in error, the while He gave them His promise to preserve it in truth.

"Moreover it is recorded in the same place that: After this mony of His disciples went back, and walked nae mair with Him. Do we then read that He recalled them, lest they should be deceived, not perceiving that He spake but in a figure? Nay, but lest they should think He spake but in a figure He had already confirmed His words with these: It is the spirit that quickeneth; the flesh (meaning thereby man's natural and carnal apprehension) profiteth nothing. *The words that I have spoken to you, they are spirit and life.*

"And yet again, when He instituted the Eucharistic Sacrifice, afore His Passion, it is recorded in the Gospels how He took breid, and blessed, and brake, and gave to His disciples, saying: Tak ye, and eat; *this is My Body;* and how, after, He took the chalice, and gave thanks, and gave to them, saying: Drink ye all of this, *for this is My Blude of the new testament,* which sall be shed for mony unto remission of sins—words usit in the Mass every day at the Consecration, in obedience to His injunction: *This do for a commemoration of me.* This too, the heretics are fain to say, was but a figure; thus asking us to believe that in that solemn moment, afore He entered upon His Passion, Our Blessed Lord again deceivit His Apostles, with a figure. Thus too taking away from that scene in the upper room the only Meaning that would explain and justifee its solemnity.

"But I do not cite those passages, brethren, in order to prove to you what ye already ken and believe, since ye are of those who, not being madmen, would rather believe God than man. I cite them in order to show beyond ony possibility of doubt that in denying that Christ is Really Present in this Breid of the Altar the heretics fly full in the face of the very Scriptures on which they claim to base themselves.

"Now we maun ask .. Why? Why are the heretics, wha dispute amang themselves ower every bone of doctrine, united as ane in baying against *this* doctrine, a doctrine not alane always and everywhere taught and believit by the Kirk, but also maist plainly affirmed by the Scriptures? For men wha believe in God, and that the Scriptures are from God, there is nae *reasonable* cause that they should not believe this doctrine. Why then do they all with ane accord, and that vehemently, refuse to believe it *against reason*? That they are offended is manifest. But *why* are they offended? What is there in the doctrine that they should be offended at it?"

Ninian Kennedy answers the question by projecting a soul into the situation of a confrontation with the Blessed Sacrament or Consecrated Elements, that is to say, with Omnipotence, Holiness and Humility. The effect on the soul will be in accordance with its condition. Even for the soul "full of compunction, contrite, humble, restorit in charity" it will be awesome. For the soul "full of pride, wanting in charity, in contrition and the purpose of amendment, with sins unrepented, unwillant—above all, unwillant to bend the knee," it will be intolerable. "What will take place in the soul of such an ane brought here intil the Presence of Holiness, as of Humility and Omnipotence? He will ken full weil in his inmaist heart that he should smite himself on the breist and cast himself doun in abjection of self. But because he will neither abase himself nor, not doing it, abide the Presence of Holiness as of Omnipotence, he will *will* Omnipotence and Holiness to be far away from him. There will be a rising up in him of hate—aye, and to violence—against that Presence of Holiness that makes him less than nothing, for all his pride. And so as he cannot deny the necessity of the celebration of this Mystery, since it is maist straitly enjoined in Scripture, he will devise for himself—or embrace with joy and a feeling of being greatly let free when he finds it professed by others; he will embrace because of its evident "truth"—a doctrine accordant to the which it is all but a Figure, and he need have no fear, no sense that he is come to judgment since what he is in presence of, what he partakes of, is but breid. (Wherein indeed they speak truly of their ain sacraments, since their celebration of them is invalid and unlawful.)

"And sae the unanimity and violence with the which all kinds of the heretics assail this particular doctrine sae plainly taught in their ain Scriptures, point on their very face to pride as their first source. *Which is to say that their rejection of the doctrine is but a means whereby their pride and unregenerate will seek to protect themselves* against the Divine Holiness, Humility and Omnipotence, Whose living touch would shrivel their pride to dust."

(Pride—the word may pass for the moment though it is at best the first turning of the key in a double-locked door: most of our key terms by which we think to understand ourselves and others are out of date or in need of further definition in terms of the actual personality-event.)

"This at least is manifest," he concluded on this point, "sae lang as this Presence is in this hoose built by man for God, sae lang will the silence of God be louder here than the voice of man. But if man rid himself of the silence of this Presence of God, there will be nae voice here hereafter louder than his ain." Later on when the attack was actually made upon the church by the mob and the tabernacle was as always the first thing to be overset on the altar, it struck Ninian Kennedy afresh that if God was no longer to be Present in the church building, He could have no more function hereafter than to hover vaguely above its roof nodding assent to the doctrines propounded by the Reformers from the pulpit, which would now replace the Altar as central in the edifice. If the significance of the Reformation was the substitution of the Will for the Intellect, the Reformers' private interpretation of the Bible for the Authority of the Church, Wealth for Poverty as a spiritual ideal, it was equally a substitution of the Pulpit for the Altar. That is to say, the function of the Deity, as also His status, became changed. From the Creator-Being, Present in the church in Person for the purpose of being worshipped, He became from the Reformation onwards no more than the Supreme Guarantor of the notions being enunciated from the pulpit.

Similarly, the second matter has nothing to do with the question whether heaven exists and the Virgin Mary is honoured in its courts—and the other Saints likewise in their degree; if anyone holds that all the dead are simply sleeping an endless sleep of pure non-existence his belief is unaffected by the question—the question why certain men against the universal practice of their time and all times previously, against the universal "feeling" of their own and previous ages, and against the plainest injunctions of the Scriptures which they took as their sole Authority in belief, suddenly adopted—contrary to their "conditioning," that is—an attitude not merely of indifference but of active hostility towards the mother of the Founder of the religion they professed.

Let Ninian Kennedy continue.

"And now," he went on in his sermon, "what of Christ's Mother whom also all heretics are agreed in refusing to honour; claiming that they thereby the mair honour her Son—not seeing that thereby they make Him worse than the worst of men, since not even the worst of men will take pleasure in hearing his mother ill spoken of and used despitefully. . . . What do we read? . . . *Hail, full of grace, the Lord is with thee; blessed art thou amongst women!* Such was the salutation of the Angel sent by God, recorded in the Scripture. Yet the heretics, although they claim to fulfil all that is enjoinit in the Scriptures, refuse to echo it. Again, in the same Scripture: *Blessed art thou among women, and blessed is the fruit of thy womb!* So spake St Elizabeth. But her salutation also the heretics refuse to echo, though it is expressly stated in the Scripture that in speaking thus she was *filled with the Holy Ghost.* And Mary herself—not less, it is very certain, filled with the Holy Ghost—made her reply: *Behold from henceforth all generations shall call me blessed.* Here it is maist straitly enjoined

109

in their ain Scriptures that thenceforward in all times, which includes our ain, she was to be called 'blessed'—and the heretics in naething show mair clearly that they have verily putten themselves outside the company of the true Kirk of God, than in that they refuse to the Mother of Christ our Saviour that title of honour which the Scriptures distinctly state was to be given to her by Christians unto 'all generations.' We ken this, for they openly make it their boast. Our question is, *why* do all heretics, in disregard of the practice of the Kirk everywhere and in all times and of the prophetic injunctions of the Scriptures—in plain defiance of the thice-repeated utterance of the Divine Spirit—refuse and that also with vehement scorn and anger to honour the Mother of Christ? And what can the answer to this question tell us of the nature of heresy?

"It cannot by ony means be denied that in being chosen by God to be the mother of His Incarnate Son Mary was exalted in honour abune all the children of men; and it would be unreasonable, not to say impious, to suppose that the honour she had on earth has been ta'en from her in heaven. But the heretics are offended.

"Now what is it in us that is offended at the exaltation of another and moved thereby to anger? Maist certainly it is not humility. Nay, but it is envy, and cannot be aught but envy which is angered at the honour given till another and desires the douncome of all that are exalted ower us. And envy is ane operation of pride.

"But mair . . . Nothing defiled can come where God is, and it is certain from her choice and appointment to that dignity that the mother of the Son of God was not less than the maist pure of creatures. Yet we may observe that it is precisely this, her purity, equally with if not mair than the honour given to her, which moves the heretics to scorn and fury. Now . . . what can it be in us that is offending at purity? I reply that I ken of naught unless it be impurity, for there is naught else to which purity could be a reproach. If they were not themselves unrepentantly of impure mind they could never be sae offended at the purity of another. And impurity is not itself disjoinit from pride, for it is similarly ane movement of the arrogant natural self disdaining to be restrainit by what would set bounds to its effluence.

"If we have reasoned truly the unanimity of all heretics in rejecting first the doctrine of the Real Presence of Christ in the Sacrament of the Altar, second, the obligation to honour the Mother of Christ, to call her 'blessed,' points to the working of *pride* in them, showing itself in envy, hatred of another's greater honour or moral excellence, anger in the presence of that to which they owe humility, which they are ever unwillant to accord. They do not reject the doctrine and injunction for want of the authority of Scripture, wherein baith are straitly enjoined, but because baith rebuke their pride, their envy and impurity, because of their aversion to repentance in the spirit of true inward worship and abasement. That is to say that heresy, not as regards its multitude of outward forms but *in itself,* in its innermaist essence, is primarily ane event in the depths of the spirit or will, where it concerns ane operation of pride. If sae, if in its essence it is the will that it concerns, we see how it is bootless to try to understand heresy on its ain terms, by the account it gives of itself, that is, in the mony conflicting doctrines called Protestantism, for these are but systems constructed by the reason, whereas the thing itself takes place in the spirit and in the will. The true order of events would therefore be this: that *afore ever the heretics were heretics in their mind through acceptance and professing of their doctrines, they were already Protestants in their heart through pride."*

He asks: "Are they such men in their outward bearing as we might look to see them if such be the state of their heart?" and replies: "We have all of late days had ower much reason to observe the walk and conversation of them that profess heresy, for they do not hide themselves away when they may appear afore men, and ye will bear me witness that they are all men of a scornful bearing, rapt awa in contemplation of their ain secret greatness, giving respect to nane but themselves, impatient of each other man's opinion, ever exhorting only to destruction of the thing that has been built up, indifferent to every consideration public or private except their ain advancement to dominion. And with their souls filled with impurity, as we may without uncharity conclude since there is little else of which they never cease to accuse all that dare to differ from them, and it is out of the fulness of the heart that the mouth speaketh.

111

"Puir, self-deceivit, self-deceiving men, that understand not nor care to understand what the things truly are that move them in their inmaist souls; and that gang headlong towards destruction, destroying as they gang and dragging others with them! We ought to pray for such as for the weak and infirm in mind and soul— for truly from this violent, carnal-willed and bloody-minded man wha verily believes himself a sanct of God 'tis but ane farther step to yonder madman that believes himself a king! . . ."

Having now tested for truth two universal attitudes of heretics and got the answer "pride" in both cases (the word will suffice for the moment), he proceeds to test the main heretical doctrines for "pride" in turn.

"Brethren, let us not deal in merely probable opinions. The leech cannot cure the disease if he is mistaken as to its nature: nor can we hope to cure this disease of heresy which in our day ettles to destroy baith Kirk and Nation unless we first truly understand what heresy *is*, and that in the very principles in which it is constituted as to its inward nature. Our reasoning sae far has brought us to conclude that heresy arises, in the order of cause and effect, in the first instance from pride, that the heretic is suffering from an enlargement of his *self*, and per consequent of his sense of the limits of his right and power. If it be sae, if the enlargement of pride in the depths of the soul or spirit is the true beginning, moving the man to acceptance and profession of specific doctrines, *then the doctrines taken up and professed will be such as will minister to pride.*

"Let us examine the doctrines and see if it be sae. . . .

"Take first this among their chiefest doctrines, that man is althegether reprobate from God as a consequent of the Fall. The doctrine of the Catholic Kirk is that although man is weakened in his will and faculties through the Fall, through Sin, yet his nature remains in its essence guid, as it came from God, and capable of guid, since he can of his ain will choose to co-operate with God's grace ever offered to all, whereby indeed he can be truly regenerated. But the heretics say nay. Accordant to their doctrine the nature of man under Sin, since the Fall, is evil at its root, althegether corrupt, utterly incapable of ane guid work.

"Now at the first sight this doctrine does not seem to minister to pride, since it is unflattering to man. But mark its effects! We are all of us sairly limited, baith as created beings and as men in our world, baith in ourselves and as compared with others. It is our necessary lot to meet every day mony that are greater in the land, or holier in their life, or mair glorious in their gifts than ourselves; and we are compassed about on every side by their works, their memorials and monuments—as even take this kirk, which stands daily afore our e'en a witness that there have been others here mair greatly endowed in the faculty of hand and vision than ourselves . . . aye, even of a greater piety, for wha can deny those stanes were shapit with a prayer! To them that accept themselves, the place that has been given them, with their limitations, the superiority of others is a cause of admiration, of thanks to God that He has given such gifts to others if not to themselves. But to them that are unwillant to accept the limits of what has been conferred on them, their powers and place, what a reproach! —how bitter, what a cause of burning in their heart, to be reminded on every hand that sae mony are mair gifted baith in place and person—and hae been mair gifted, for the gifted of the past have left their evidences around us in the edifice of their works and of their thoughts into which we were born and are compelled with humility to dwell!

"Now see the effect of the doctrine. At ane stroke it owerthrows the distinction between mair guid and less guid in man's works and gifts, and evens the second with the first. For it is very clear that nae guid fruit springs from an evil root, that out of what is corrupt in its essence naething of merit or virtue can arise, that there can be nae excellences inherent in the works of a totally corrupt and reprobate human nature, or degrees of guidness in works where works are all of necessity evil, and that therefore the giftedness and greatness of some men and of their works are but illusions—not inherent in the men or in their works but only imputed to them by our sinful minds. See what this doctrine does for me, if I am a man that wills not to accept my place—at ane stroke it sets me free from the intolerable burden of the duty of reverence for the gifts and works of others—for the sanctity of the saints, for the loftiness and subtlety of men of thought, for the nobility of great deeds, and for every secular work of man's hand or mind that stands in evidence of the wondrous faculties that appertain to man, albeit they hae been conferred in small measure upon me. For nae langer now are these admirable or to be reverenced, in that they show that man has receivit greatness and has done great things: rather they are to be scorned and derided as the vain works of a radically sinful human nature—to be destroyed even, if I be sae minded, as themselves partaking of sin, as they must do since whatever is produced of sin must partake of the nature of sin. So it is to pride of self after all that the doctrine of total reprobation ministers, since it dispenses him that holds it from the necessity of admiration, from the duty of reverence for other men and their works. It is to pride of self that it ministers, for in plain words that he that runs may understand it means but this, that there can be nothing and nobody in the world of man greater or mair worthy than myself, but all things are reduced to the measure of my ain littleness. *If this particular doctrine does not set me up, it cannot be denied that it at least brings all things else doun."*

He paused and looked round him. . . . "Need we look farther for the reason why they ettle to destroy our kirks? A small mind, full of envy—a soul in the which pride of self and the deep-doun knowledge of its littleness are joined thegether—is bound by its condition to hate the sight of onything mair lofty, mair beautiful, mair noble than *it* can be or do, will feel what is noble and lofty a reproach and a burden not to be borne, and will ettle to ding it doun. They say they destroy the kirks because they are temples of idolatrie. They deceive themselves. The true cause is in the springs and deep places of their soul—that they will not endure the scandal of man's nobility. They destroy the kirks, in right sooth, if they but kent it, out of rage that they could not hae biggit them.

"It is even sae with the second chief doctrine of the heretics, that salvation is by faith alane, and not by faith together with love and guid works. What again does this do but bring everything doun, in the spiritual life, to my ain measure! What does it do but take away from the saints the merit of their sanctity, and place *me,* here and now, without effort, without onything achieved or even undertaken in the arduous way of salvation, on the same ground and level with them that have laboured hardest and merited maist! What does it do, that is, but take away, aye, from

114

the heroes and giants of the spiritual life, the friends of God that have scaled the heights of sanctity, all title to ony greater honour than is due to *me*, though I may be of carnal mind and have striven not at all! Such *must* be the effect of a doctrine that denies all pairt or share in the process of salvation to onything except ane act of confident belief.

"But if these first twa doctrines minister to pride by bringing everything above me doun to my measure, the third does sae incomparably mair by raising me up abune others. According to the blasphemous doctrine of Predestination, God ordains some to eternal glory and others to everlasting punishment, and that not for ony guid or ill that they have done or will do, but simply to show His Will. It needs no argument to show how such a doctrine ministers to the very heights of pride—for it needs not to say, of course, that they wha profess it aye speak as amang the Chosen and never as amang the Reprobate. What mair could the utter-maist of pride conceivably desire for itself than the place in this world and the next which those 'Elect' heretics assert has been appointed unto them by Heaven? (Nor let us be deceivit by the humility which some among them may at times affect. All is not humble that casteth doun the e'e. And that humility is nae burden to pride which consists in bowing to a Divine ordinance that has predestinated them to stand abune their fellows. Nay but—bear me witness here!—towards you and me their humility consists in saying: Give place!)

"They are the Chosen people of God, and as such they would fain play the same pairt among men in our day as the Jews played amang the ancient nations. As they are destined to eternal glory as their irresistible and unmerited destiny, sae equally it is their lot on earth to wield authority ower all men whomsoever, so that there shall be nae government henceforward save their dominion, and all that will not bow down before them nor yet suffer their doctrine shall be putten out of the world like sae mony Canaanitish idolators.

"Pride! Say madness rather! For what is it but madness when bakers and shoemakers claim not alane to sit abune the sancts in heaven but to owercast the temporal dominion of kings

115

and governments by virtue of ane privy whisper in their lug informing them they are no clay of common men but God's Chosen Anes afore the making of the world!

"True, afore men they base not their claim upon that privy whisper. For their authority they hae another doctrine—that the haill revelation of God is in the Scriptures, and only in the Scriptures, and—mark it weil!—that *they* are the oracles of the Scriptures. God, they say, has hidden all Truth in a Buik, and has sealed the Buik—and the keys He has given to *them*. Again see how it is to pride of self that this doctrine ministers! Men never claimed such power as they claim to themselves—nothing less than a special revelation, direct from God, to them alane, in a particular light or spirit of interpretation or divination whereby they stand abune all men and alane are able to declare the Will of God! Moreover they claim that what truth God has privily given to them, that is, their private opinion, they have the right, nay, mair, the duty to compel all other men to receive from them. That makes them—Reformers ever zealous to reform not themselves but others—show as but tyrants in disguise, wishful to play the despot ower all men under a cloak of a profession of pure doctrine."

He applies a final test: "'But let us make yet mair certain. . . . If it be pride of self that is served by the gaining of the doctrines, then it will be the satisfactions of pride that would be lost by the losing of the doctrines. Let us therefore ask . . . what would be the state of this heretic, this Elect baker, without the doctrines of his heresy? It is easy to see that he would suffer on the instant a mortal douncome, to become aince mair precisely what he *is*. Still a baker—and nane the waur o' that!—but nae langer ane Elect baxter with authority from God to knead men and not breid. And sae equally with them all: without their doctrines they could be naught but simply what they are, as their birth and natural powers have made them, such men as we ken them . . . among men, compelled to look up to mony of higher place and greater mark; as regards gifts of mind and nature, compassed on every hand by others and the works of others incomparably better endowed, making them show as they indeed are, silly and inferior; as to theology, compelled to remain dumb, as having neither authority nor learning; regarding temporal authority, able only to wield it at hame—if sae be they can rule their ain wives.

"To such insignificance would they be brought down by the loss of their doctrines. Whereas, the doctrines given them, the lowest in the land is instantly lifted up abune the highest, the morally worst is instantly superior to the morally best and with a higher destiny, the dullest of wit is instantly mair glorifeed in his stupidity than the best endowed in his intelligence.

"They may think, puir self-deceivit wretches, that they have discovered the doctrine hidden from the ages, and that it is the jewel of pure truth they carry in their heids—but this apple of doctrine grew in Eden, and what they have perceived is nae divine light but the gleam of pride and of concupiscence.

"*While without their doctrine they are naebody, with it they are gods, having authority ower all men in a world in which there is nothing greater, because nothing is permitted to be greater, than their selves.* Such is the effect of the presence of the doctrine in their mind, and I trow we have not missed the essence when we say it is also the *real* even if uncomprehended *cause* of their acceptance of it. . . ."

We leave Ninian Kennedy continuing his sermon, shortly interrupted by the arrival of the Protestants to destroy the church, when, as anticipated, their first act was to overset the tabernacle on the altar. In the course of the melee he was struck and knocked unconscious—leading him to say to John Tod on a subsequent occasion, touching his face with rueful tenderness: "That's the strongest theological argument you Protestants will ever hae, John—a blow on the heid!"

117

VIII

The genesis (of the interior personality-event: which Ninian Kennedy called "pride") is in *confrontation*. Not as a notional encounter but, anterior to all rational structuralising, simply a confrontation of *being* and *being, being* brought into the presence of *being*.

Such confrontations are taking place continuously every day in everyone's life. The *being*, "I," finds itself constantly and continuously confronted with an "other" *being*, whether in the living form of other actual persons, or in the apprehension of them in something they have done or made and on which they have in consequence left the imprint or lingering presence of their *being:* and this confrontation may be actual, as it were face to face, a confrontation of *being* in an actual person living and present or in the actual works in which the "other" *being* has left himself present, or it may be in the form of an unrationalised recollected apprehension of the "other" *being* either in a recollected living personal presence or as recollected present in his works. Such an encounter in recollection is equally a real confrontation.

Every such confrontation of *being* with *being* must produce a result. There can be no such thing as a neutral encounter between *beings;* if there is no result there has been no confrontation. Either there will be a merging, an embrace in the sphere of *being*, or there will be a rejection. But this is not at all as with particles in the material universe, whose *nature* it may be to attract *or* repel each other. Such an occurrence in them implies a mutuality of effect and activity—the particles attract or repel *each* the *other*— whereas in the confrontation of *being* and *being*, one is always the *being*, "I," the other another *being* which is simply "there." (The situation is not affected by the fact that the confrontation may be between two *beings*, "I"; that simply constitutes a double confrontation.) Secondly, and considering everything simply from the point of view of *being* as such, it is the *nature* of *being* to be apprehensible, and therefore one may say that in every confrontation the *natural* result should be an embrace and interpenetration of *beings*, so maintaining the universe in its ontological integrity.

But the *being*, "I," is not only a being which apprehends, it is also a being which *wills,* and it is therefore open to it in any confrontation, in despite of that nature and integrity, to *reject* or *repel* the other *being*—with a *Nay,* as it were, in place of what the situation demands by its nature, a *Yea.* That is to say it is open to a *being,* "I," in any confrontation with an "other" *being, to will its non-being.* This is the un-*natural* act which breaks the integrity of the universe.

That such an act is truly or, better, really—*i.e.* at the level of real *being*—un-*natural,* contrary to its own right nature, is evident in that by doing so the *being,* "I," diminishes itself, that is, as a *being.* Someone has said: "Whoever affirms the self, also and by the same act of necessity affirms the not-the-self, and of course conversely." In the terms we are using this means that the *being,* "I," affirming, that is, saying Yea to or embracing at the level of *being* an other *being,* is interpenetrated by that "other," becomes one with it, is enriched by it in the degree in which in a sense it *becomes* that other. To say Nay to—that is, to *will the non-being* of—an other *being,* is to be impoverished to the extent of the non-absorption of that "other" into the *being,* "I," or self, the remaining apart from or outside it.

The loss is not limited to the privation of the negating "I" or rejecting self, but is in a sense limitless, or co-terminous with the universe of *beings.* The whole universe of *beings* is held together by a Yea: by a Nay its unity is shattered. If the negating or rejecting of *being* by *being* were to become widespread this could only produce a sort of anarchy in the universe of *beings*—[shortly thereafter some men might begin to wonder what was happening, what had gone wrong with their society].

The reason for the rejecting action on the part of a *being,* "I," is simple, like every event at this level. *Beings* are of all magnitudes, like stars. Inevitably therefore many overshadow or alternatively outshine others. Surrounded by other *beings* as such, therefore, the *being,* "I," is confronted with their magnitude or brilliance, and this magnitude or brilliance—very, very often their *greater* magnitude or brilliance—has to be affirmed—or rejected. The Nay-say or negation, the refusal to embrace at the level of *being,* to merge and be interpenetrated, occurs when a *being,* "I,"

119

confronted with a *being* of greater magnitude or brilliance, experiences that magnitude or brilliance not as a matter for affirmation or ontological embrace, but as a diminution of the "I," as involving the burden of a comparison not to be borne; and to free itself from what it experiences as an intolerable diminution, rejects the magnitude or refuses the effulgence.

To have the will fixed at a constant Yea in respect of every other *being* whatsoever—an absolute, invariable affirmation—would define the condition known in another terminology as *sanctity;* it would be to be made *real* by interpenetration by the reality of all other *being,* or illuminated by every *other* effulgence. To have the will fixed at a constant maximum of Nay-say, the *absolute* rejection of all other *being,* would be a scarcely possible human condition: it would be the condition known in another terminology as *hell;* even to approach such a degree of negation in ordinary life would mean to be in a condition severely psychopathological. The great mass of us, most *beings,* "I," go on from moment to moment, amid continuous confrontations, with our will wavering between part-degree affirmation and part-degree negation, Yea and Nay succeeding each other in varying intensity as the moments pass. (A bogus and quite unhelpful kind of seeming affirmation has to be looked out for: it consists in vigorous or intense Yea-say to an other *being* after an unobserved identification has been made between the other *being* and the *being,* "I"; in other words what we are performing here is not an objective act of affirmation of an other *being* but all unsuspected a subjective act of admiration or approbation of our self.)

The situation is illustrated in a simplified form on the opposite page.

All this has taken place of course causally before a single rational idea has been formed; it is all strictly pre-notional. There is the confrontation of the *being,* "I," with another *being,* and instantly the movement of the pointer-indicator to one side or the other, towards affirmation or negation. *Subsequently* there will arise in another part of the mind *ideas,* whose function it will be to "explain" the primary or first reaction *in rational terms.* The *being,* "I," will now at once "recognise" in this newly arrived idea the reason *why* he reacts to such-and-such another *being* as he

120

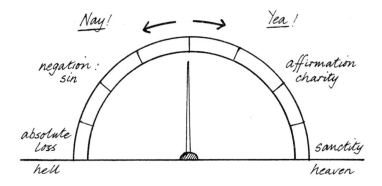

The pointer-indicator shows the will in a state of equilibrium, *before* a confrontation. At the moment of confrontation with an "other" *being* it will move instantly to right or left, towards affirmation or negation—*must* do so; there is no such thing as neutrality when an "other" *being* is in confrontation; what is called neutrality or indifference is a form of negation.

does. He will now feel *justified* in his reaction, because he has now been provided with *reasons* for it.

And those "reasons" will now and thereafter be the basis for his action in regard to the "other" in question, notwithstanding that they are not in fact the *real* cause of that action, the real cause being the pre-rational will-movement which still remains out of rational sight. (If we are in the least sincerely gifted with the quality of introspection, of watching what is happening in ourselves as we think and feel, we can easily see this at work: we can see how every day and again and again and in all sorts of contexts we are half-way from impulse to action before our "reason" for that action occurs to us, accompanied often by a great feeling of relief, and thereafter remains the justification for that action although in fact it is not at all the true or first cause of it.)

Now, most importantly, coming to the crux. . . . If a rationalisation which justifies a total or sweeping negation of everything in man, nature or the supernatural which has been burdensome or diminishing in its effect in confrontation of the *being,* "I," (such as a doctrine of the total reprobation of man and nature, the essential evil of the non-"I," or of justification by faith alone, *i.e.* without the necessity of the burden of affirmation of the non-"I")—if such a doctrine-rationalisation be presented over a particular area all the Nay-sayers, rejecters and repudiators, all those who have felt the greater brilliance or magnitude of other *beings* like a personal diminution, all of that state of will in that area will instantly "perceive" the "truth" of such doctrines and will rush to join themselves to those who are propagating them. Nothing will exceed their enthusiasm or "sincerity" or sense of freedom following their "illumination," so that they will find it intolerable that others should still exist not holding the same obviously true doctrines or in other words still according their Yea-say to *being* of a brilliance or magnitude from which those "believers" are now justified by their doctrines in withholding their affirmation.

Another sketch, on the facing page, roughly illustrates what has *really* happened as a personality-event.

The infinite range of human potentiality
and achievement in the glory of creativity —
everything
fine, high, noble, distinguished, magnificent —
intellectuality, contemplation, mystical knowledge,
The _Real_ Presence of God, God as Reality, not concept,
Beauty as Truth, etc., etc.

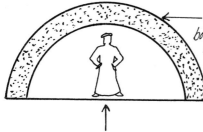

— the impenetrable
bomb-proof 'shelter' of
Reformation doctrine,
negating all above
under 'uselessness
of works' total
'reprobation,
radical evil, etc.

The Protestant '_free_' in his Kingdom, i.e.,
'delivered from' all the above: nothing is
'above' him because nothing else is doctrinally
'there': nothing of the above can get in at him
to reduce him; making him the most
important and interesting _being_ existing.

123

Part Two

Part Two

I

"He stretched his legs out in front of him, turning his feet to the blaze. The warmth from the red fire in the midst of the wide fireplace stone-carved all about was less than the warmth within him. This inner warmth, released by that of the glowing fire, bathed him in waves while with arms on the wide arms of the chair he leaned at ease. Turning his head slightly to one side while he pressed it against the high, carved back of the chair, he let his eyes wander up and over the flowered tapestry hanging beside him. The tapestry covered the walls of this snug chamber; scarcely a draught made the figures on it seem to stir in their depicted pastoral. Warmth mounted on the room. . . . There could be no doubt about it, all that coldness in the outside-himself, formerly not to be subdued by a fire's heat, had given way, had passed away to warmth that lapped the uttermost of sense, and flowed from verge to verge of consciousness. And that estrangedness that used to be in the 'out-there' had ebbed away and left things solid and familiar all around him: that one-time hardness that, freezing and pressing, smothered the flutter in his breast, had gone, and now—and especially here—he was surrounded by a benevolence in things, turning as it were their mild, accustomed face towards him. He had had to come here—to this room tapestried, all warm from its wide and sculptured hearth, to this wide chair carved like a throne —to encounter and recognise himself, to meet his *real* self, as it were to keep a tryst with his identity. And he felt how *right* he must have been. Howsoever storm-troubled with hesitations those first steps, he now basked in the proof. The Truth shall make you free, said the Scripture. And he *was* free, boundlessly free. The Truth had made him free. The Truth had brought him *here*."

In other words, by means of the Reformation's success, John Tod had realised his life-long *unconscious* objective—that of attaining a point where his adult situation could be made to reproduce his position in his earliest and most formative conscious period, when everything was turned towards *him* as the centre, with warmth and deference, in uttermost security, and he was the biggest thing in sight, his word the Truth for everyone around—a position which deep-inwardly he always thereafter felt to be his due. He is sitting in the bishop's chair, in the bishop's chamber, now *his*, and now once again all are compelled to tremble at his "truth." Most visibly, most palpably the Truth has made him *free*; and this freedom and his superior situation are permanent as unassailable, for to his joy and his secure assurance he can reflect that they are guaranteed by God.

To him in his beatitude and fulfilment enters, like an apparition, Ninian Kennedy. Emaciated and in rags, racked with the cough of a wasting disease, he is a figure of offence to John Tod in his respectable plenitude. He has been "on the run" and in fact long supposed to be out of the country, but has come as he says "this last time" to argue out with John Tod the nature and final effects of his Reformation.

As considerations of space have now become most stringent, I omit the novelist's measures to heighten and maintain the drama of the encounter, as also the whole of the preliminary sparring except for one or two points which require to be elevated into attention by reason of their essential relevance and almost total omission where the Reformation is referred to elsewhere.

The first concerned an accusation of Ninian Kennedy's that the Reforming leaders were "nocht guid Scots" from the outset. Buchanan is the only one known to have spoken Gaelic as his native tongue although it was then still the principal language of Scotland; the rest were of an already partially Anglicised element in the population. Knox had lived in England, married an English-woman, ministered to an English congregation abroad, and had he died earlier would have been a figure in English rather than Scottish history. His contemporaries upbraided him with his not speaking good "Scots" but as they put it, "knapping the Suddrone," *i.e.* speaking Englishman's English. He was already in fact not a true Scot at all but a North-Briton and like many such persons since, sent his sons to England to be educated and brought up as English-men. The success of his party signifies the appearance on the scene of a new type, not simply Scottish traitors in English pay (there had been plenty of those formerly but they had still remained Scots or Albannaich, members of a nationality of distinct entity and autonomous status), what now for the first time appeared upon the scene was the type of the Scot as a *northern provincial Englishman,* although speaking as yet with the accents and to a diminishing degree the vocabulary of what had once been a distinct and autonomous language. The Reformation was set up and paid for by the English Government and by the expectations of material gain on the part of the "unprincipled hyena" class of "famished" Scottish nobility, and that is how and how alone it came to be established. We are at liberty to think, as we were all brought up to think, that the Reformation was "a good thing," but that is how it was actually set up and had it not been set up in that way it would never have been set up at all. Had the Reformers not had the assistantce and support of those two elements they would have shouted for a time and then died away, their doctrines being too repulsive for the at least moderately-affirming element who normally make up the generality of any population.

This is very far indeed from the picture that has always been presented to us of an entire nation—except for a few wilfully wicked whures and idolaters—with instantaneous joy and from the purest motives welcoming the bright light of unsullied doctrine poured down upon them from the new pulpits by a number of "grave," "earnest," "thoughtful"—though never, it is true, "learned"—men. John Tod attempts to raise this point—of the alleged popularity of the Reformers—only to have it answered by Ninian Kennedy's pointing out that the only popularity the Reformers enjoyed was with "the hound-rabble that would bay for onybody that would tak the muzzle off them." A mob of the lowest elements of a population can be raised anywhere at any time by simple assurance of indemnity for their acts of violence, looting and destruction. Such was the mob which followed the Reformers from place to place destroying churches and ecclesiastical edifices, and of such was their "popularity." But as someone has remarked, "where you have a mob you have a mob-master, and where you have a mob-master you have a paymaster." The technique is much thought-of and practised today, in particular perhaps by the Communists and in Communist countries, where the "organiser of spontaneous demonstrations" is a trained and valued agent of the Party's activity. But the Reformers thought of it first.

It is essential to realise that the Reformers and their convinced followers were at the time of the actual struggle a very tiny

129

minority—who had almost certainly never even been heard of by the majority of the population. The struggle was over and the Reformation established before the people in any but the restricted area where it was a struggle at all had even heard of it, let alone become acquainted with its doctrines and passed judgment upon them. With the exception of a few individuals as, for example, Erskine of Dun and Argyll, and a particular place like Dundee, it would be true to say that the entire area north and west of the Tay—the majority of the population in those days —had either never heard of the Reformers and their doctrines or were indifferent or hostile to them. And even in the central belt where they were known because of their violent activities the "armies" that took the field ostensibly on their behalf were feudal levies dragged out by their superiors, and so uninterested in the conflict or actually hostile to the Reformers' aims that they took the first opportunity of straggling off home and leaving the French and English to fight it out; while those who could not withdraw from the situation because the conflict was actually in their territory—as in Leith—showed where their sympathies lay by helping the French to load their guns and stoning the Reformers out of their boundaries. So much were they a minority and unpopular that even with the monopoly control they at once seized over the entire educational system and even by the recruitment of "baxters and cordwainers," bakers and shoemakers, into their ordained ministry, there were many years after their triumph still scores of parishes up an down Scotland for which they could not find an incumbent.

At this point the debate passed naturally on to the question of the zeal of the Reformers for learning, for education. And when this is mentioned we really do feel on strong ground. For surely there is about this a quality of the axiomatic. All our lives we have found it universally accepted that Protestantism meant disinterested zeal for education—to cure the "darkness" and "ignorance" of what went before. It is as certain as that the stars move in their courses.

In reality it is the most preposterous claim of all. Even in one's early years one was conscious of some vast fallacy embedded in this universal assertion. "Learning" and "education" have a humane sound; the "worthlessness of works" of a "totally depraved nature" has not; indeed it has the opposite. Humane learning and total reprobation of human nature cannot in fact be reconciled or made to live together. How on a personal level could the Reformers have been characterised by a zeal for learning when (if we except George Buchanan's Latinity) none of them had any of it to speak of?—still more when on the general level reprobation of the Reason and Intellect and all their works was a prime element in the Absolute Negation of all human excellence and achievement which was the essence and effect—as it was the cause —of the Reformation as an actual event in actual human personalities? How could the Reformers' joy on the realisation of their Election have been combined with an equally upspringing enthusiasm for the works of Reprobation and the Reprobate?

As for the "darkness" and "ignorance" of the times before Protestantism, truth compels me to admit that I have more than once felt a deep resentment at the waste of years of learning-time and opportunity enforced upon me by the conditioned delusion that was my "education." When at last by my own efforts and as it were by chance I caught sight in the distance of the majestic edifice that was Mediaeval Thought and Culture, I realised in a moment that as a product of "Scottish Education" I had all along been nothing but an ignorant provincial and cultural hobblede-hoy—and the gall was in the fact that somewhere or other deep down within me I felt I had all along known it or suspected it (just as I had all along known a certain shame for Scotland in the meeting of any of its dignitaries with the representatives of free and actual nations of an actual culture, lest their essential provincialism be too clumsily apparent). This particular "dark" and "ignorant" notion about pre-Reformation Christendom goes in fact beyond anger and almost all the way to laughter. The Reformers ascribing—or our ascribing on their behalf—ignorance and darkness of mind to the minds and creative spirits of pre-Reformation Christendom is something like a Lilliputian imput-ing dwarfishness to Gulliver. In more equivalent terms it is like being taught all one's life on every hand as a major fact in the truth about history, necessary to be apprehended, that the Ancient Greeks were a completely unlettered, uncultured people—and then discovering Aeschylus.

What then is the origin of this extraordinarily well fixed notion about the Reformers' zeal for learning? It was certainly not a zeal for humane learning, for philosophy or the arts, all of which were anathema and works of the Devil. Yet a zeal for something there certainly was. What was it? In reality it is perfectly simple and easy to understand. It goes back to the fact that the Reformers were a very small and unpopular minority. If they were to survive as a party and their doctrines to be perpetuated they *had* to find a means of conditioning future generations to acceptance of their views. What they had therefore was not a disinterested zeal for learning but a very interested zeal for indoctrination, for the "brain-washing" of each next generation: the substance of their "education" was their doctrines. The Reformers' zeal for "learning" was a course forced on them by the necessity of their situation. The Nazis in their day, the Communists in Russia and elsewhere in Europe, the Chinese, recent One-Party Dictatorships that we have seen arise, any and every minority revolutionary group taking power anywhere—none of those could possibly afford *not* to have as an immediate ideal "a school in every parish."

(This of course is not to deny that the love of learning traditional in Scotland survived the Reformation or that as the generations passed on many individual Scottish Protestants, despite their indoctrination with a negating attitude to the humane arts, while outwardly conforming, privately and illicitly—it would have had to be illicitly—took delight in the culture of the Classical past *for its own sake*. But that is not quite the point, is it?)

Those matters even so belong to the "historical" or backward-looking aspect of the Reformation, and what we are coming down to in this section is its "essential" or forward-looking aspect, the element that entered into time.

John Tod challenges Ninian Kennedy as to his having gone about saying, referring to the future, that the doctrines of Protestantism having entered into and taken possession of the mind, must needs produce a confusion in the soul, which confusion must equally of necessity emerge in an equivalent disorder in social life and the historical process of society. What did he mean by such statements?

"*Ye* will tell *me* that, John," said Ninian Kennedy, and, leaning towards him . . . "Let me ask ye. . . . How do ye conceive Truth?"

John Tod perked up.

"Needs not to ask it. *We* hae the Truth. Our Faith is Truth."

The other gave a faint smile, as if hearing what he had expected to hear. He then asked . . . "How then conceive ye Freedom?"

"I hae tauld ye already. It is the Truth that makes us free. *We* are free. Our Faith is Freedom."

"And Justice . . . how do ye conceive Justice?"

"Justice is the establishment of the Truth, which is our Faith" —with condescension—"How else could ye conceive Justice?"

"And a right social order, John. . . . How conceive ye that?"

"A right social order is ane in the which the truth and justice are maintainit. That can only be ane social order under the rule and governance of our Kirk, which is appointed to maintain truth and justice."

"And how conceive ye now Scotland?"

John Tod, with a snort—"Scotland is but the community of the Saints . . . what mair could it be hereafter?"

Ninian Kennedy gave a tired smile, and nodded, recognising the answers he had anticipated. . . .

"Now ye must admit, John, that when ye make truth, freedom, justice, the nation, equal simply to your religion and its regnancy, ye give to all these concepts a meaning they never had afore."

John Tod shrugged . . . "We give them their true meaning."

"Ye cannot deny, nanetheless, that in your minds all these concepts have been transformed, and hae lost the meaning they had in all time formerly. . . . Heretofore men might dispute about truth, but they aye understood it as something to be established by the mind conforming itself upon its objects; as independent therefore of *my* feeling or *your* opinion—as correcting indeed all judgments that partook of private feeling and preference by submitting them to be judged by the object. The meaning *ye* give to truth is althegether different; simply, *whatever is prescribit by your Kirk.* . . . Likewise with freedom: men have aye kent till now not alane with their minds but in their bodies what it is to live in freedom, and what to be in bonds. Nations also were in bonds when their enemies had dominion ower them, in freedom when they were answerable only to themselves in their ain country and lived freely accordant to their ain traditions as a nation. But *ye* make freedom equal only to the Protestant religion; *that* is freedom. . . . Sae also with justice. Justice was aye supposit to consist in this, that every man—and God first, it needs not to say —should receive his due. *Ye* make it mean something althegether different, althegether new: simply the regnancy of the Protestant religion. Scotland too, that was till now a community of men and women of common blood and inheritance working in common under God and by His Will for the informing of life on earth with the especial quality of their 'mind' and 'way' embodied in their tradition, ye would turn henceforward to mean nothing mair than sae many persons holding the Protestant religion. And upon other such concepts that men live by and that shape their lives ye work a like transformation.

"Now the effect of those transformations of meaning, though it may be hidden from you, will yet be seen. If your religion be a lie—and I ken it is a lie, if only by the token that I hae seen ye make it yourselves—then ye make men to believe a lie thinking it to be the truth, and thereby will cause them to forfeit in their ain life and their societies' the fruits of truth, and to suffer in their stead the disorderly fruits of a lie in the mind; unable to escape the fruits of the lie because believing that their lie is truth. Freedom, for instance . . . our Scottish people will aye cherish freedom mair than life itself; if now they come under your tutelage to identifee freedom simply with the Protestant religion they will be ready to follow the Protestant religion to the death—or worse, to the loss of all true freedom. By means of such a transposition as ye hae made in the meaning of freedom, ye might gang about to subject our nation entirely to England—as I foresee—while they still supposed they had freedom, and even mair than ever, sae lang as they had—if it was all that they had—your Protestant religion. And for justice . . . under your new transposition of its meaning ye might work the greatest injustice—as your Party hae already done, robbing the poor and giving to the rich—while all rest assured that justice reigns sae lang as your religion bears the rule, and even that there was nae true justice until you came.

"Sae with all the other ideals . . . men will nae langer ken under your new dispensation how to realise them, since they will nae langer ken how, rightly, to conceive them. And sae, attempting to realise all ideals in the belief that they are comprisit in

134

your religion, they will reap, it should be manifest, not the fruits of those ideals but in their stead the fruits of your religion. *They will reap, in effect, nothing but the final effects of your doctrines when they hae worked out their true nature and displayed it in the lives of men and societies and nations. . . .*

"And that these effects of their ain nature and inner necessity must be damnable I clearly foresee."

John Tod said, gibingly, "Are ye also amang the prophets?"

"Nay, John, prophets there be nane among us, though amang you I ween there be mony. . . . But if things be truly comprehended according to their nature. sae also will their effects be foreseen afore ever they be brought forth."

It all seemed brittle and of no consequence, to John Tod, and from a man of no account—logic out of a heap of rags (he had already suffered in himself the Protestant transformation whereby he regarded his own state of superior material well-being as a sign of God's favour and the truth of his doctrines, and poverty and rags and social unsuccess as a sign of wrongness and divine reprobation).

"Prophesy to us then!" he said, with taunting assurance, as it were stroking his chest with his broad red beard. . . . "Show us the end of our doctrine!"

II

"Its end it to be perceived already," said Ninian Kennedy, sighing, "and must hae mair and mair enlargement in time coming. . . . For see . . . by your doctrine of faith, in the which ye put doun the intellect and allot its place to the will, ye hae sown the seeds of division. As indeed ye do in general and not alane in matters of faith, by the contempt that ye hae and loudly profess for the intellect or reason, which ye are wont to call ane whure of the Devil. Sae lang as the intellect had the primacy, not alane in matters of faith but in everything that concerned truth, it was a means of uniting men. of making men *ane*: for the operations of a faculty common to all, working by its ain principles which are independent of all, in the apprehension of truth which is abune all and the same for all, could not but work for the uniting of all, and that the mair the mair it was leaned to, the stronger it was in itself, and the mair it was rectifeed by being lifted abune the passions and all private elements, which by reason that they are private work for division. But ye, Protestants and heretics, when ye make faith equal to trust and not intellectual assent, and when, owercasting authority, ye choose out to yourselves doctrines accordant with your preference, and when in general ye put doun the intellect from its appointed natural primacy in the apprehension of truth, thereby exalt the personal *will* and enthrone it: and thereby ye commit men to be guided by ane errant private guide which. by the reason that it is private, must needs set men at odds thegether.

"For the will in matters of truth is blind. If it be not guided by reason it must be guided, or rather led or impelled, by the passions and desires, and as these acknowledge no law save the law of their satisfaction, and that a private and not a common end, the result must of necessity be the breaking up of the unity of all Christian men, which unity was rooted not alane in a common acceptance of ane external authority in faith and morals but in ane universal common assent to the authority of the intellect rightly usit and conformit to its proper ends."

John Tod said: "All sic intellectual pish and tush is weil called by Paul in the Scripture 'philosophy and vain jangling'."

"Nay, John, what he that ye with ower-great familiarity call Paul designated as vain jangling was never philosophy pursuing its proper work which is truth, the apprehension of ends, but the sophistical quibbling engaged in for its ain sake, or out of vanity, or for gain, as was much done in those days lang syne. Sic men were condemnit for making use of philosophy for personal, other-than-philosophic ends—even as ye heretics. as I understand your case, use religion for personal, other-than-religious ends—some of ye, like your freend Pitfourie, in full scornful deliberation; others, the "sincere" amang you, without kennan fully weil what it is that they do."

"Ye may rest easy," broke in John Tod. "We will unite all men with our doctrine and under our governance."

"Will-they-nil-they? Nay, John, even among the generations to come whom in what ye call your zeal for learning ye will make it a chief work to protect from the evidences of the Faith of Christendom to the end that they may grow up to ken naught but the doctrines of Calvin, even among them there must ere lang arise those that will turn your principle of the private will against yourselves, that will take liberty to refuse your authority, till in the end the Christian world be broken intil as mony pairts as there will be individual men able to maintain or impose their private will in the context of things religious amang their fellows."

"Nay, nay, John, the plain sodger will ettle to be a captain yet "We'll take order with them!" said John Tod threateningly. in spite of ye, and if he cannot be a captain in your army he'll even hae an army of his ain, though it were but small. Sic is the human nature ye hae let loose, and ye'll not govern it for lang. Your persecution will not halt it, for naething lifts a man up with less merit or effort of his ain than his public persecution, and sic is the force of the passion to be foremaist that mony would be ready to perish by persecution for the sake of that maist exquisite moment of delight when they would be the absolute centre of all men's e'en, a moment that naething in them would win for them any other way—all the while, it might nanetheless be, in the conviction they were victims on the altar of truth. . . .

"And therefore the first and continuing fruit of your religion everywhere it has free course must of necessity be that which the Scriptures plainly say is the fruit of the flesh and not the spirit,

137

that is, *sects* . . . sects and the bitterness that is aye joinit to sects. Sects must multiplee and war thegether even to the death for the power to force acceptance of their private doctrine upon all. Wars I foretell, and that the centuries aheid will be drooned in the blude of the strife of sects; and my heart is wae for those mony and mony thousand innocent yet unborn wha will yet lose life in the bootless fruit of your seed of quarrel. And, the sword apairt, innumerous hearts bruised and broken in their tenderest strings, for the sect sets houses against themselves, and there will be father against son, and brother against brother, from generation to generation."

History at least promptly verified that part of his prognostications. Wars there had been before between Europeans, the result of their imperfect Christianisation, and no doubt when that Christianisation had been carried farther they would have had an end—Christianity had tended and was tending even to humanise war, if such a phrase be possible—but prompt upon the Reformation wars burst out of a bloodiness and a ferocity and on a scale unparalleled in the Christian centuries; the element of religion introduced a bitterness that was something new in slaughter. The centuries following were little more than a bath of blood—and, so far as religion really was an element, all for doctrines on the Protestant side to which few men coveting a reputation for humanity would care today to be known to accord an intellectual assent. And wars of blood apart, and coming right down to the present day, countless millions of personal tragedies in the wars of sects—parents who "would rather see their son dead" than joined to another religious community, and so forth. Even where my own small Evangelical communion was concerned my recollection is full to this day of the agonising conflicts in families and the hearts of individuals when someone's "untheological" conduct or opinion split the community from the Antipodes to the haughs of Echt.

"But there is division far mair radical than opinion that ye work, in the soul. . . . In aulden times . . . afore Christ . . . men were aye found bound in chains in their minds by the force of ane certain idea, whereby they were able to think of man only as a twa-fauld race. To the Jews all others were but the Gentiles,

138

shut out from Promise: to the Greeks there were but the Greeks—and all the rest outside in the wilderness of Barbarians. Even the Roman citizenship, though men might pass intil it, was a division across the world of men and a cause of thinking of men as twa—and of treating them as twa. And as ye ken, in all times and generations it was taken as a thing in nature that men should be of the twa kinds, bond and free. Whatever the principle of division it was the habit of the mind in all auld times to conceive the race of men as, afore all things else, apportioned in twa orders or kinds, ane superior by its nature, ane inferior, ane glorious by its destiny, ane shameful: ane therefore ordered and destined by its nature to bear the rule ower the other, which might by nae means avoid that governance since it was in its nature for it to be subject.

"That world-auld division of man, with all the oppressions that were bound to be done when there were twa kinds owing naething to ane another save to rule or be ruled the ane by the other, all that, the pride of the dominators and the groans of the oppressed, and their life without hope because their state was fixed, it was the effect of our holy religion to do away. In Christ there was now nae mair Jew and Gentile, Greek and Barbarian, bond or free: all were made ane Man in the shedding of His blude for all, ane ae-fauld humankind, of ane equal standing before God and ane equal hope of heaven.

"Now ye with your doctrine of some that God ordains without merit to eternal life and others ordained without demerit to eternal punishment, *have undone that work of Christ,* and by your separating of all men into Elect and Reprobate hae brought back the aulden idea of man as a twa-fauld race, inheriting a twa-fauld state on earth and a twa-fauld destiny. Man that was made ane by Christ is made twa again by your doctrines. And not only sae, but mair fixedly than ever afore; for the former divisions between the twa kinds, not even the circumcision itself, was ever as impassable as the great gulf fixed by God between the Elect and the Reprobate.

"The necessary effects must be among us ere lang. When man became Ane he became subject to the law of love, without possible exception of ony because all were of ane paternity, all equally redeemed and in hope of heaven: all became answerable

139

under the law of love for all. But there is no law of love that can bind twa immutably separated kinds of men, and now again the only justice is that ane should rule and ane be ruled by the other. The Elect, therefore, are by God's ordinance given the rule at the same moment as they are set free from all obligation under the law of love towards them that will be under them; and it needs nae special knowledge of our human nature to foresee the outcome. The effect of Predestination is to raise up a company filled with the consciousness of God's especial favour, supposing themselves under command from heaven to rule the rest, to whom they owe nothing under the law of love. But as it happens, the Elect under God's dispensation are maist notably the rich and powerful —or them that ettle to be sae by the exercise of their Election! Moreover they believe another doctrine, that guid works are of nae merit—conversely that evil works are of nae demerit: nane of the Elect can ever be damned for onything he may do upon the Reprobate—that is, in general and in effect, the poor and defenceless—in the exercise of his God-ordained rule over them, and—I recall to mind—in obedience to the divine injunction given by the prophet Calvin, wha has commanded ye, I hear, to get rich! Mark further that the abandonment of all inward restraints on the abuse of inferiors comes in at the same time as the owercasting of the external restraints provided in the Catholic Kirk's ordinances against the oppression of the poor, which it ever enforced against the rich and powerful whenever and wherever it had scope and freedom. Mark all these things and consider the end to which they point. For me, it needs nae garment mair prophetical than these rags to foretell that the effect of this Reformation must of necessity be such a setting-up of rich Elect, and such oppressions of the poor Reprobate, as have never been seen since Christ. The voice of the future is nae cry of joy that raise to heaven when mankind kent itself Ane, but the lamenting of a wretched humanity that they are sundered again into Twa, and the groans and cries of generations doomed to toil without hope for the benefit of God's Elect."

It may at first be a cause of astonishment and some difficulty to realise that the Reformation state and character of mind and the doctrines based on them represented in reality a re-assertion of a condition of soul which had existed before Christianity and from which it had been the achievement of Christianity to rescue the world; that (in this sense) it represented an undoing of the work of Christianity. It ought to be less surprising that Protestantism, and Calvinism especially, led directly in the order of cause and effect to the social conditions of Capitalist exploitation—less surprising because the connection has often been pointed out before, and because Protestantism at the time such exploitation was unquestioned as to its moral rightness, and booming across the world, itself gloried in its paternity. As Ninian Kennedy showed, such a development—a division into exploiting and exploited "classes"—was *bound* to be the social effect of the activity of men believing mankind to be two-fold, and themselves "Chosen."

"Nor are oppressions all," he went on. "For ye cannot set bounds to the flight of ideas once ye hae let them loose. They will follow their ain course from mind to mind and take up their abode where they will, *alangside what other ideas they may find there before them.* Now, the idea and sentiment of *the tribe* or *nation* is sic an ane as will be found in possession when the ideas and sentiments ye have let loose have time to gang abroad, and will inevitably be encountered by them in the minds and spirits they will inhabit. What will the effect be when they join thegether? Remember that your Reformation has shattered the bond of Christendom and set the nations asunder; the nations that aince kent they should stand side by side in a greater Unity, now stand over against each other in a posture of defence or of aggression. What will be the outcome. think ye? when your new-auld idea of the twa-fauldness of man, and the other idea that ane of the twa divisions is Divinely Chosen to fulfil a higher destiny and to dominate the other, come thegether and are joinit to the idea and sentiment of *the tribe* or *nation*? Do ye not see the danger fast impending that whatever remains over of what was aince a Christian state of man, after your Reforming devastations and the wars of sects, may perish althegether in the resultant wars of mutual destruction between nations that feel themselves Elect, 'Chosen' to dominate all others?"

(This dialogue was written, as it happens, during the last War).

As John Tod did not reply, Ninian Kennedy eventually continued reflectively. . . . "Ye ken, John, I believe that ye will never root out from the hearts of men a memory of the distant light of freedom aince brought to the world by the Catholic Kirk, howsoever dim a recollection of the teaching that in the eyes of God the slave is equal to the Emperor, that the poor are even His special care, and that while He will resist the proud His heart is open to the humble . . . and therefore in the oppressed a dim consciousness that their sufferings are unlawful and their oppression contravenes a higher justice. . . . See now that if in consequence the moral indignation of the poor and oppressed should be kindled at their state, it will awake not in a world filled with the Catholic consciousness, that man is Ane, but in a world that *your* doctrine and spirit will hae filled with the idea and the sentiment that man is by state and nature Twa. (Sic an idea is even of a nature to appear specially self-evident to the class of the oppressed by reason baith of the unity of their common suffering making them feel *ane*. and the univocal witness of the great gulf atween their state in the world and that of their oppressors, wha are self-evidently of a different 'kind'.) If therefore, now, the idea of the twa-fauld nature of man—and ane of the kinds Chosen, the other Reprobate—should be joinit in the oppressed with their sense that their state contravenes a justice above the justice of their society—should be joinit with their deep-doun recollection of aince having heard ane authoritative Voice declaring the poor specially beloved in some Quarter abune the human—an ower-easy transposition would soon make *them* the Elect, the specially beloved, destined to rule, and their oppressors, sinning against the higher justice, the Reprobate, wha by appointment should be subject. . . . Aince let them become possessed of that idea, and their moral indignation, resentment at lang-endurit wrangs and bitterness of recollected misery—with the inspiring sense that *you* have now of being instruments for the imposition on the world of the order fore-ordained by Destiny—will provide the power on their pairt for a warfare that will be for nae redressing of injustices but the extirpation of their oppressors or the making them the oppressed in turn. . . . Should such a social war take place your Elect would perish by a judgment on your ain ideas. . . . And wha can say also whether—the wars of Elect nations apart—the fragments of the Christian and Catholic order that survived your fury and the application of your misconceivit principles, would not be swept away in such a blind avenging flood!'"

If here Ninian Kennedy seems to have adumbrated a connection between the Reformation and certain violent social events that have taken place at the other end of Europe in our own lifetime, and which from considerations of place alone would seem to have been unconnected, have patience and all will be explained. The connection is in fact intimate, *though not by way of direct causation.* For the moment let us continue with the effects of the Reformation as foreseen by Ninian Kennedy. He went on to claim—

"There is a seed of mair present ill, forebye strife and blude and oppressions, that ye hae sown with your doctrines . . . and that is the seed of sadness—aye, of despair. And the falseness of your doctrine is in nothing better seen than in this, for the true Evangel was to bring men hope. . . . Ye ken that in the ancient days men were sair holden in their minds under that auld idea that they called *necessity, anangke* as the Greeks had it, and groaned in spirit because they thought their destiny was written for them in the stars or some sic heathen superstition, and that they strove in vain against a judgment delivered already upon them by their gods. And that haill world of auld time burst the bonds of its despair, and casting away the shackles of 'necessity' rose up rejoicing in the freedom and hope brought to men by Christ.

"The sorrow of that bondage to necessity, the sorrowful sense of being bound by ane higher Power to an immutable fate, ye hae brought back again to be a burden on men's souls. In this also ye have undone the work of Christ, returning to the auld things that were already done away, with your doctrine that all men are ordainit to their ain place in the next life afore ever they were born into this, and that nae guid work, nae virtue nor striving can avail to change aught of our allotted fate, but we are bound utterly and constrainit by a destiny that recks naething of merits as of deserts. How much the mair sorrowful above measure they whase unjust destiny it is to be numbered among the Reprobate from God, without hope of moving Him nae mair to justice than to mercy. . . . But even among the Elect, if a man had a pairt yet of natural kindness within him how could he not be sorrowful to see sae mony, though better than himself, ganging their waeful gait to everlasting torments!

"Aye, and your doctrine, not alane that guid works are of nane avail for salvation, but that the nature of man is itself radically corrupt and incapable of ane guid act, but that everything a man does with no matter how pure intention is utterly vile and stinking . . . what a doctrine to make a man despair in the midst of his labours in his weary life! Ah, John, this world that we but press under our feet in leaping out of the abyss of non-being into the abyss of God, but that by the operation of love might be turned into a garden for the time of our sojourn here, ye hae turned into a prison, with yourselves as gaolers ower all men till they be ready to be damned. Fareweil now to joy! For myself I declare to ye that even if the faith of Catholics was ane error, as I weil ken it is not, I would rather dee now in that merry fault than live my life nae matter how worldly well in all the future that may yet be yours!"

There can be no doubt about the gloom: it arrived promptly with the imposition of the doctrines just as it was a natural product of the radical Nay-say that lay behind the doctrines. A description of its spreading effects is better left over however till a later context.

Meantime John Tod finding Ninian Kennedy remaining meditatively silent at this point, tauntingly urged him to continue with his list of evil consequences of the Reformation.

"Surely . . ." he said, "surely ye hae not gotten to the end! There must be *other* evil consequents of sic an evil cause!"

"There *is* another probable end"—Ninian Kennedy looked up at him—"worse it may be in certain wise than all others."

"What is that?"

"That men might lose faith and the inward posture and formation of religion althegether."

John Tod made a sound indicating incredulity. "That could never be! To believe is natural . . . and therefore necessary!"

"Sae it is. Like health to the body. Yet it may be lost even sae. And the lang disedifying of the warring of sae mony sects,

144

each ane accordant to itself the sole possessor of the Truth—did it consist of but its prophet and a twa-score followers—sae mony ill deeds done in the name of true religion, sae much malice, injustice and absurdity attributed to God by minds of small capacity and little learning making up their ain theology, might weil at last gie cause to mony to doubt that *nane* hae the truth, that truth in religion may not be kent, or even that there is *nae* truth in religion. . . ."

John Tod ejaculated, still sceptically—"How would men live their lives syne—without religion?"

"The necessary effects of the loss of siccar belief are easily foreseen," said Ninian Kennedy. "They are the loss of all that is founded in belief. That is, firstly, morals. For religion gane, morals have nae siccar foundament. With loss of firm faith there must come the loosing of ethical as of theological restraints and an uncertain rule in all that concerns conduct. Men will become their ain judge of what is right or wrang in their behaviour, if they lose not the sense of right and wrang in behaviour althegether. . . . And—mark this weil!—as the laws and commandments of God are not something arbitrarily imposed on man from outside or above, but are *written in his nature* by its structure and constitution, men must therefore suffer in themselves and their societies the consequents of their acts in breach of the commandments, *whether they ony langer rightly ken them to be laws that they break or no.*

"These consequents are in the discordance and weakness of the faculties of the soul—whase harmony in the strength of correspondence with the commandments of the Creator, which are therefor their ain laws, is the perfection of man. That is, in the first place, the *Mind* becomes weaker, not alane in its authority but in its operations in everything that concerns judgments, and men will therefore become darkened in their perception of what things are for their guid and the guid of their societies, and judging wrangly will follow harmful courses. That other faculty of the soul, the *Will* likewise, afflicted with weakness, inconstancy and indirection, will hae less power either to avoid evil or to conform itself to such guid as is still perceived. . . .

"I foresee therefore that from the loss of belief alane, and the decline of morals consequent thereon—from darkened judgment

145

and the multiplying effect of sae mony acts in breach of the law of God—from this internal cause alane, haill societies might be made ready to perish. . . . Certain they would stand in danger of perdition in that doubt and darkness of the mind, irresolution and enfeeblement of the will, the weariness of life, the hopelessness, aye and despair that afflict societies without faith that hae gane astray in sin, would make them poorly able to resist a peril from without—as, it might be, the attack of a class or nation that felt themselves 'Chosen' to rule ower all the world."

A little before John Tod had been delighted to think of an argument that should demolish the whole of this. He said, with a tone of triumph, as already seeing himself the victor in the argument—and over such an antagonist! . . .

"In all that ye hae said ye contradict yourself. If men in the end reject our Kirk and our doctrines, how will such things arise in later times, being the effect of our Kirk and our doctrines? Answer me that, man of reason as ye be!"

The grey figure did not have the appearance of being greatly overborne by the logical point. He did not even look round at John Tod but half-musingly said, as if disposing of an irrelevance or lesser issue. . . . " 'Tis not the doctrines nor your Kirk's governance *in themselves* that will bring those things to be, but the 'mind,' the condition of the soul, that engendered them in the first place and that they in turn engender, the formation they give to the soul, and which they then let loose to work its effects in the world. . . .

"That that 'mind,' the same condition of soul that is in you, can be present and active in the world when you and your Kirk and doctrines are not, is evident, since as I hae shown ye the world was full of a consciousness of mankind as twa-fauld, a conviction amang some of being 'Chosen,' over against others that were 'Reprobate,' a sense that life itself was evil and fit to be the ground of nae natural guid, and that the haill of life was overshadowed for guid or ill by a destiny that fixed men's ends, and sae forth—everything that marks your ain soul, your ain 'mind' upon life—lang afore ye were ever here—lang even afore the religion of Christians was in the world, or the Christian Scriptures written in the which ye claim to have found all this. And

146

by the same token such a 'mind' and condition of soul could equally well prevail and remain active in a society that had left your Kirk and your doctrines by the road or even nae mair professed the Christian name.

"For, ye see, all that—your doctrines and your Scriptures and your Kirk—hae been as it were but a mask putten on by that auld 'mind,' that auld formation in the soul, for fear its true, un-Christian face would frighten away even yourselves in a world that has a lang time been Christian—just as the same 'mind' wore mony masks of doctrine and mony names in days lang gane bye. It is, in fact—this 'mind' that is in you—nae mair new than it is auld, nae mair auld than of the present time, but a shape and condition of things in the soul that may form itself there in ony age, in onybody—but which becomes fixed from one generation to the next when it shelters under the form and justification of a system of ideas claiming the sanction of truth, as with your doctrines and theology, and a society or Party to guard and transmit it, as in your Reforming Kirk. But it is the shape of things in the soul, the 'mind' upon life, which is the substance, and therefore fitted to survive the dissolution of such accidentals as forms of doctrines, and kirks and parties. And it is from this surviving shape of things in the soul that the effects are produced that I hae foretold.

"For the soul being by its nature active, by its activity limns its ain features upon the outer world of its society, since it can assuredly limn nae others: and sae the character of a human society cannot be other than as the character of the human souls and 'mind' whase activity brought it into being and made it what it is. Thus, the effect of the activity of men that look on man as twa-fauld—whether they belang to your Kirk or never heard its name—cannot be other than to bring to being in their society a sharp division between twa classes of men; men that act, feeling themselves as 'Chosen,' whether they call themselves Christian or not, will soon, in the measure that they have power, bring into being a 'Chosen' class, and another class feeling themselves to be 'Reprobate,' for they will be treated as such, and not in charity and justice; men that conceive there is nae merit in guid works will do nane, and will make for themselves a society free from guid works, that is, full of injustice; a society made up of souls acting in

147

the conviction that they are not creators of their own destiny but althegether under compulsion of higher powers, will never be adorned with the marks of freedom, the works of man's free creator spirit, but only by such works as they conceive they do under the calling of necessity—such as to rule others, or to get rich—or to make shoes. And sae forth. . . .

"That is wherefor it is not necessary for men to continue to hold your forms of doctrine or to be ruled by your Kirk in order to produce the end effects of your doctrines: it is only necessary they be descended by their spirit from men that were once formit in their souls by your doctrines through being once subject to your governance. Your Kirk may lose its power ower men to the last iota, your doctrine and theological formulations cease to command their belief and allegiance, or even ony mair to be current among them, yet the formation of their soul remain behind, the 'mind' upon man, his state and destiny, the way of looking upon life, the lying of their will towards life—and the resultant shape of men's acting in society and towards their fellows—that ye will hae brought back with the establishment of your doctrines."

John Tod exclaimed impatiently—"Ye are beside yourself! Do ye now confidently assert that all that ye hae foretold will surely come to pass? . . . that as ane effect of our doctrine, the reformation we hae wrought, the poor must be oppressed, syne at the last rise against their oppressors with violence, that there must be wars between nations thinking themselves to be Elect—as if there were ony Elect save the Sancts!—and that the societies of men, if ony there be left remaining after such conturbulations, must die from within by the weight of their particular and general sins—even though they no longer ken them to be sins—and from despair through the loss of faith and the sense of truth! Pish, man! do ye now confidently assert that all that must surely come to pass?"

Ninian Kennedy looked at him. "I am no foreteller of the future. What will assuredly come to pass I ken nae mair than you. . . . What I do assert is that such is the nature of the 'mind,' the formation of the soul that lies behind your doctrines, that engendered them and that they in turn engender and let loose, that if and where they are established and take free scope such will be the outcome—*must* be, since it follows from their nature as the stane falls earthwards."

148

III

Here we leave the novel. But we leave it when Ninian Kennedy has opened up the kernel of the situation in having drawn a clear and essential distinction between what he called *the Face* and *the Mask*.

The Mask was the system of Reformation doctrines, it was the organisation of the Kirk, it was the account the Reformers gave of themselves, it was even what they *consciously* knew or thought was going on in them: all this was no more than a Mask, and that is why practically everything that has been written about the Reformation up till now has been beside the point, most of it quite worthless from the point of view of understanding the Reformation in its essence and in itself, and that is the reason also for the feeling of disappointment, of not having penetrated to the essence, of remaining radically unenlightened or "coming out by that same door as in one went," which was a clinging sense in reading accounts of the Reformation, thunderous or moving or seeming to be clinical as they might yet be. Instead of identifying the Face, they dealt only with descriptions of the Mask, which was in reality something secondary, an epiphenomenon, no more than the true event's contextualisation in the sixteenth century. The true event, the Face, was the condition in the personality or soul or psyche illustrated in the sketch on page 123, the essential Nay-say to all reality which in confrontation with the *being,* "I," was experienced at the first or most instantaneous level as an over-shadowing, this Nay-say from the depth of the will having risen high enough in the personality for events in consciousness to begin to form or shape themselves on it, in such fashion that it eventually emerged as an apparatus of judgment and a cause of action.

This it was, this condition in the soul or psyche, which caused the effects of the Reformation; the Reformation itself (*i.e.* the shape and character of the Reformers' consciousness, the system of doctrines, the organisation of the Kirk, etc.) was only the *means* by which it caused them in the particular conditions of the sixteenth century; that is to say the Reformation was only a means by which a condition in the primary, instantaneous consciousness, an event in the metaphysics of the will, enabled itself to impinge on reality at the level of events, both internally in the individual conscious life and externally in action in society. The events of the Reformation as a religious occurrence, that is, were only the *means* whereby a primary movement in the depths of the soul— the Nay-say or repudiation of the non-"I" which is of no time or century or rather of every time and century—caused affairs in the upper world of consciousness and in society to constitute themselves in such a fashion as to provide it with scope and freedom in the conditions obtaining in the sixteenth century. Once that impulse, that Nay-say from the depths, had obtained scope and freedom the means whereby it attained it might later on wither away, in other words the doctrines might be discarded, the Kirk abandoned, while the effects continued, as Ninian Kennedy was at pains to point out, since the doctrines, the Kirk organisation, the formally Protestant consciousness of the Reformers were in the first place only a *means* and the *cause* of the whole thing lay elsewhere. (That is how it comes about that a whole generation today can be ignorant of the doctrines, and would repudiate them if they knew them, and have to all intents abandoned the Kirk, *while nonetheless retaining a deep recognition of a real identity with the Reformers in what they were about.* It would be perfectly logical for a completely irreligious man of the present day to recognise such a perfect identity with the Reformers—thousands do—since it would simply require in him an apprehension however dim of the identity of their pre-fully-conscious impulse and condition with his own.)

The whole of this and also what follows will be easier to understand if we pause to consider the process by which what was originally a movement in the primary area of the consciousness or "instinctive" level of the soul, a movement right down in the metaphysics of the will, than which nothing can be more basic, comes to be a part of the upper or clear consciousness, clothed in an ideology or system of doctrine, and thereby a cause of action in the personal and social world. How does the Mask come to be fitted to the Face: that is, how does an "instinctive" movement in primary consciousness become something in full consciousness; how does such an event in the personality as is illustrated on page 123 come to be a system of doctrine and a basis of action;

150

what is the psychological mechanism whereby the first becomes the second, that is, whereby a subconscious event in the metaphysics of the will becomes a conscious system of belief leading to action?

The mechanism is in reality quite simple. Of course, so far as getting rid of all obligations whatsoever towards what is not-the-self is concerned, a simple doctrine to the effect that human nature is totally reprobate or evil would amply suffice: as we have seen Ninian Kennedy point out, the effect of such a doctrine is to disembarrass the self at one stroke from the obligation to acknowledge the superiority in act or being of anyone else whomsoever at any time or in any age: the *being,* "I," becomes immediately the equal at least of every actual or conceivable *being,* not-"I." And such a reductive mechanism had in fact been used again and again since long before Christian times, conjoined to and made effective in the many forms of Gnosticism and Manicheeism, before it appeared again in the sixteenth century with the doctrines of Protestantism as its means, this time, of effective entry into the upper world of consciousness and action.

But the soul is by its nature active, and after all the reductive mechanism of a doctrine of the total evil of things was not required so that the soul might rest in the contemplation of its equal depravity with all other beings; on the contrary its use was as a preliminary step towards an aggressive movement of the *being,* "I," into the area of *beings,* not-"I." To effect this aggressive entry a simple mechanism is called into play. To understand it we have only to recall what was said much earlier about the mind approaching reality and, in the attempt to cope with it, reducing its complexity by means of the application of *categories* of its own manufacture, which I think we likened to a number of labelled sacks into which we stuff realities as we encounter them, afterwards thinking that we know the realities because we know the name on the label on the sack. If now we approach reality-not-ourselves with only TWO sacks or categories we simplify reality in the easiest and crudest way by the simple process of dualising it, that is, separating it into no more than two divisions. This done, it only remains to carry out the further gambit, now also familiar to us, of transforming concepts and transvaluing values so that they adhere exclusively to *one* of the two radical categories, which

151

in consequence now appears shining with an absolute commendation as against the other which is now black with an equally absolute reprobation, and the stage is set and the justification provided for an absolute aggression of the "Chosen" or "Elect" category in which all virtues inhere against the other category from which all value has been abstracted.

Such a mechanism working in the personality has many times in the past been the link between the Nay-say at the "instinctive," primary or instantaneous level of experience and the conscious debouching of men of "Chosen" category upon the active stage of history, where they appeared armed with a system of doctrine —the Mask—serving the purpose of justifying their "Chosen" status and activities in ideological and verbal terms which recommended themselves to their contemporaries to the extent that they had a valid-sounding because familiar-sounding ring to the ears of their particular age—armed in addition it might be with the swords and other actual weapons of their age, for men of a "Chosen" category have not always been content to rest in the contemplation of the superiority of their status and actual "kind" to that of other men, but not infrequently set forth to establish their actual superiority in the objective historical field. The natural consequence of the bursting out into history of men, *first* of primary Nay-say at the metaphysical level of the will, *then* of "Chosen" category in a mentally strictly dualised world, *finally* of systematic doctrines to justify and rationalise all, was bloodshed in their aggressions, and of course destructions, often fearful bloodshed and destructions.

The Mask then requires not only a strict dualising of reality, the strict division of reality into two rigid categories in the mind, but also and finally—to make one of the categories glorious and deserving to be triumphant—a system of doctrine which will recommend itself by the consonance of its terms and concepts with the pre-occupations and associated terminology of the age. That was why the bursting out of organised Nay-say, of institutionalised and justified aggression of so many *beings,* "I," against *being,* not-"I," in the sixteenth century masked itself behind a form of religion and religious doctrine: not otherwise would either the

Nay-sayers or those who were not, the Reformers or their opponents, have been able to think they understood what was going on; the sixteenth, like its preceding centuries, having been a time when human life and everything connected with it and its activities was supposed to be explicable only in terms of theology and religion.

But time passed on and preoccupations changed. As Ninian Kennedy had foreseen, the long disedification of the wars of sects —I am speaking of course not alone of Scotland—came in the end not to the triumph of one sect, still less to the establishment of truth, but to exhaustion, disgust, and in many quarters to hesitation, doubt and scepticism where the truth of religion was concerned. It all ended in the eventual relegation of religion to a place apart from the main preoccupations of life, to its transfer from a public to a private region of concern. By, say, the mid-nineteenth century a Nay-say to reality not-the-self by the means or method of religion could have led to nothing more socially convulsive than individual membership of some sect—of "Chosen" membership, it need not be said—where one would rest in the sense of one's "Elect" consequence and the repudiation of absolutely the whole of reality that did not concede it.

But by that time grandiose schematisations that partook of the nature of both history and philosophy had come into fashion, replacing religion as explaining man's situation and his destiny, and it would have been natural and no surprise had a movement of essential Nay-say from the depths found its way on to the plane of conscious formulations and endeavoured to aggress at the social level by means of a mental dualisation of reality bearing the labels of historico-philosophical concepts on the two categories and putting forward an historico-philosophical system of doctrines behind which to advance in the actual social world.

In point of fact the nineteenth (and twentieth) century turned up a perfect case. The categories and doctrine system of Communism form a perfect nineteenth to twentieth century counterpart of the sixteenth century Mask; the perfection of the counterpart being due to the identity of the Face the Mask in each case covers and conceals.

First, as always, there is at the immediate level of consciousness the confrontation with *being,* not-"I," and the negating or, in

153

terms of the end proposed by the movement in the metaphysics of the will, the annihilating of it; emerging in a doctrine not this time that the individual soul of man is utterly reprobate from God, since this is not pre-eminently a religious age and such language is out of date, but in the doctrine that *human society itself is utterly reprobate* (by reason of the Original Sin of exploitation), utterly reprobate from History. The terms of the doctrine are secondary, of the age: what is essential, and identical with what occurred in previous times, is the sweeping, all-inclusive negation of the action of the will, freeing the individual to the uttermost from every obligation of obeisance to every "other" and the works of every "other," to in fact all reality, not-"I," and incapable of contributing to the "I," whether contemporary reality or of the past, to the uttermost past. The holder of such a doctrine, miserable and disinherited as he may be by social condition or personal endowment, is at one stroke entitled to look with contempt on all existing reality as representing merely the achievements of or participation in a Reprobate Society. "If this particular doctrine does not put me up, it at least brings everything else doun."

The effect of the doctrine, identically with the effect of the Reformation doctrine of Total Reprobation, is to free the *being,* "I," absolutely from all obligations towards or recognition of its being overshadowed in the total area of *beings,* not-"I." That is the wonderfully liberating effect of the doctrine—*freedom not to have to acknowledge.* By the doctrine of the total reprobation of non-Communist society the Communist is at one stroke set free from the past, equally from the present insofar as it is not Communist. The essence is not in the objective truth of the doctrine as an account of history but in the radical inward liberation which accompanies it and which he shares in identical sort and degree with the reprobating sixteenth century Protestant. Furthermore, as with the Protestant, it is the desire of or impulse towards such a liberation, however subconsciously it is present and at work, which is the *cause* of his conscious "recognition" of the "truth" of the doctrine. He immediately "recognises" the "truth" of a doctrine which at one stroke sets him free of all obligation to every overshadowing reality or "other" whether of the present or the past. The Communist by the effect of this doctrine at one step stands above history and all it has ever contained, so much so that in fact the only conceivable function or value of history has been to produce *him*; it has had no other and could not conceivably have any other: similarly he stands apart and free from and "knows" himself of a different and superior "kind" to his whole contemporary world.

For of course the next step has already taken place. Society, or the outer reality, has been divided in the mind into two categories in a dualism of the strictest sort. There exists only the Proletariat, that is in effect the portion of the "working-class" that has been indoctrinated with Communism, on the one hand, and on the other all the rest: the Proletariat who are "Chosen" not by God since religion is "out," but by "History" which is another way of saying the same thing, and all the rest, who are "capitalists," "bourgeois," or whatever the term in fashion may be, but who are in any case out in the wilderness of the Rejected of History and due only for liquidation as their just meed. Once again, as in the days of the Reformers, all who are not of the "Chosen" are the Reprobate whose just lot it is "to be putten out of the world like sae mony Canaanitish idolaters."

For the final gambit also has been played. The transformation of concepts and transvaluing of values. Truth equals not Truth but Communism and can never mean anything else: Truth can never be contrary to Communism; Freedom means not Freedom but Communism and Communism exclusively; Justice means not Justice but Communism and is otherwise meaningless; Peace means not actual Peace or the tranquillity of Order but the triumph of Communism, and till Communism has triumphed Peace has not been attained. Art is tolerated only insofar as it is useful for propaganda and involves the conception not of Art for or as Art but a transconceptualisation, Communist-Art. Morality too, as with Reformation Protestantism, has in every traditional sense disappeared—the doctrine of Total Reprobation necessarily abolished it, made it illusory if not actually evil—"he preached an ethical sermon"—and has been replaced: as with Reformation Protestantism Morality meant and could only mean quite simply "anything which is in accord with and advances Protestantism," so with Communism Morality is inconceivable except as meaning "anything which is in accord with and advances Communism."

155

(As an example of the completeness with which the transvaluation and trans-identification is extended to cover every form of permitted activity, the *Sunday Times Magazine* of 10th October 1965 notes that "Sport, like everything else in the New China, is inextricably bound up with ideology. Even her world-conquering table-tennis team were told to "learn from the writings of Mao Tse-tung," arm themselves with ideology and remember that table-tennis was a revolutionary endeavour." So that now in China there is no more table-tennis *as* table-tennis, but only Communist-table-tennis. The fusion is characteristic.) Moreover, as with Reformation Protestantism, Communism as a means of its realisation accords the highest ethical position to that supremely ego-aggressive emotion, Anger.

In other words here we have again the one category shining with an *absolute* commendation, the other black with an *absolute* reprobation—the simplest possible aspect under which to present "Truth," and of immediately "obvious" attraction to minds small whether by nature or the accident of the deprivation of the means to breadth, especially when joined to a disposition to resentment. By the simple process of becoming Communist entire masses of the most primitive people become at one stroke superior to the most sophisticated, Black (should it feel inferior) at one step becomes superior to White, Asiatic similarly to European, the deprived individual to the most wealthy or cultured, the man of poorest mental endowment to the man of highest intelligence, exactly as with Protestantism—superior and *in an absolute way*, from which there is no appeal, since those categories are eternally fixed—not by "God," as once, but by "History," which in the mental event is exactly the same thing. ("God" and "History"— the internal event is identical. Each represents nothing more than the appeal to or invocation of a *Supreme Guarantor*.)

Communism, in short, not considered from the point of view of its doctrines and contemporary terminology which are strictly secondary and derived from the conscious and rationalising part or function of the mind, but from the point of view of its innermost essence as an event in the area of the deepest and most instantaneous activity of the will, has an absolutely identical Face with that of Reformation Protestantism; it is in its deepest essence in the personality an identical event.

That is why all "learned" and "scholarly" work on Marxism or Dialectical Materialism whether by avowed Communist "philosophers" or others is beside the point and can never bring us to an understanding of the phenomenon—as much beside the point as has been all the "learned" and "scholarly" work on the Reformation and Reformation doctrine and what the Reformers said or actually thought about themselves. The essence of the matter in both cases lies elsewhere—in a negating movement of the will, an impulse to be disembarrassed of the "other," which in itself is characteristic simply of man, of man everywhere and at all times, a movement which is in short of no particular time or place—except that from time to time in this or that human area circumstances have been favourable to a running-together of numbers of such wills, which by the process we have followed may emerge on the actual stage of history organised as a party and advancing behind the Mask or banner of a system of doctrine couched in such terms as the age will find relevant-sounding and therefore carrying an air of validity because seeming to be consonant with widespread contemporary notions of what are the basic or ultimate concerns of human life—in the sixteenth century religion, in the nineteenth and twentieth a mixture of history, philosophy and economics.

The correspondence between Bolshevism and Reformation Protestantism, apart from the doctrine-system, the Mask, is extraordinarily close—the identity indeed; for ONLY THE CENTURIES BETWEEN KEPT THEM FROM BEING THE SAME THING.

Each on the basis of its starting point in a Nay-saying movement in the depths of the will was a Party which seized despotic power by force at a favourable moment of history. Each to secure its perpetuation immediately made itself *an educational dictatorship penetrating into the remotest and most intimate regions of the private or personal life*—for each the individual had no status or function thenceforward except to be the subject of indoctrination. The membership of both had and has the identical sense of liberation coming from their disembarrassment of the whole of overshadowing reality, the whole of *being* that did or does not concede or reflect their superiority. The membership of both enjoyed and enjoys the uniquely exhilarating consciousness of being the designated instruments of ineluctable Destiny, whose joyous duty it was in one way or another to effect the liquidation of every unaccordant element. (And of course the effect of both, it must not be forgotten, was necessarily enormous bloodshed and destruction, amid countless personal tragedies.)

On the side of their exterior effects both *automatically,* that is, by the operation of the system itself, brought to the top everywhere throughout the societies they created limited men of violent negating will; such was the type of man who automatically came to dominate their societies at every level. Men of large acceptance and affirmation, if not liquidated, escaped if they could; if they couldn't, stifled. (As Burnes in his day stifled, even after two hundred years of unopposed power had blunted the extreme rigours of the regime and made it bland by comparison with its first ferocity—just as individuals of large acceptance and affirming impulse still stifle if the accident of their circumstances should condemn them to upbringing in an Evangelical sect or to residence within a territory where such a sect strikes the note of society.)

Not without good reason therefore did Ninian Kennedy prognosticate gloom as a following condition to the establishment of a regime based on such a soul condition as lay causally behind Reformation Protestantism. In point of fact a fetid sort of gloom seems to have infested even the joy of the "Chosen" at the very moment of their triumph. In Germany at least not only an invincible melancholy but even suicide was a persistent and disturbing feature among the early Protestants, and the same phenomenon is to be observed among Bolshevists at the time of and following their success. (This need occasion no surprise. The act of Naysay at the primary level of will-events backfires as it were into the personality. This is because whoever negates the not-the-self also and by the same act negates the self. The misery of such a soul comes from its separation from what is negated, from the breach of the ontological unity of the universe of *being.*) Among the "Reprobate" gloom was of course an inevitable effect of their consciousness of their condition, but it was and is, for the above reason, a marked feature of the mood of the population in general and at large. In Scotland the period since the Reformation has been marked at every stage by a phenomenal exodus of the population of whatever degree of indoctrination, while in our own days

158

the Communist societies within reach of the non-Communist world are only able to retain their population by dint of walls, armed guards, electricity and dogs.

The parallel in external things could be extended. What we have to keep clearly before the mind, however, is the initial and interior identity. *Neither Communism nor the Reformation can be understood until it has been perceived that initially and in the metaphysics of the will they are identical phenomena.*

(Here it is certainly not out of place to mention an incident of peculiar aptness. John Knox died in the midst of a thunderstorm, in an ecstasy—one imagines, because thinking it was he who was making the thunder. As the thunder rolled he raised his hand and contracting the fingers shook it above his head. In other words, with complete symbolic aptness, the Father of Scottish Protestantism died giving the Salute of the Clenched Fist.)

Early in 1936 there appeared a small volume called *The Future of Bolshevism,** by Waldemar Gurian. It passed almost unnoticed: all the same it ought to have been in the hands of all statesmen and politicians, educators and everyone desirous of understanding his world; and this is true equally today, when so very much of the consideration of current problems and the decisions taken with regard to them are haunted and falsified by crucial misapprehensions with regard to the past, particularly the more recent past. Gurian, at the time a world authority on Bolshevism, showed with great clinical intelligence what practically no one else had perceived at the time, and probably even fewer realise today—that German National Socialism, far from being as it appeared a contrary or opposed system to Bolshevism, was in fact and in essence identical with it—was indeed, if one may so put it, a "purer" form of Bolshevism, insofar as it was as it were less hampered by having to carry along with it a cumbersome and complex piece of ideological furniture like Marxianism (a very heavy and solid Mask indeed).

But Ninian Kennedy had long before pointed out what must inevitably happen when the inner mind-formation characteristic of and in its time productive of Protestantism—the concept of the

* Sheed and Ward.

"twa-fauld nature of man, and ane of the kinds 'Chosen,' the other 'Reprobate'"—came into conjunction and fused with the concept and sentiment of the tribe or nation. In that case the "Chosen" would immediately become the tribe or nation itself, or rather those members of it who possessed or were imbued with the consciousness—and in due course the doctrine—of its uniqueness in the sense of being in an absolute way superior, of a different and special "kind," separated by an unbridgeable gulf from all the rest outside in the wilderness of non-membership; whom moreover it was the "Chosen" race's inevitable and joyous Destiny to subjugate or put out of the world.

The pattern, or progression, is by now all too familiar, indeed classical. First—the origin of the matter—is the confrontation with the "other," and the movement of repudiation or negation in the will at the primary or immediate level of consciousness. Then the conceiving of human reality under the aspect of only two exclusive categories, the strict dualisation of everything human by the mind. Then the attachment of all positive and value concepts to *one* of the categories, making the one category *absolutely* of value as against the other which is now in an absolute sense reprobate or repudiated. And finally the theory or doctrine-system —in this case "Race" theories and theories derived from "History" as establishing the superiority of the German nation as such— justifying all this in the rational or idea-forming region of the mind. Or we should have said, in this case, finally the violent bursting out on to the field of history of men who had undergone such a process and become imbued with such ideas, their violent struggle being an attempt to compel human reality as it *is* to conform to the actual inner state of their *will*, externalising itself through their theories and ideas.

It would be heartening had it not escaped notice that we have met all this before much nearer home. In mediaeval times all those who lived next to the English found them bad and aggressive neighbours*, by reason of the fact that their ruling (Norman)

* "Over many centuries and until quite recently, the English treated the Irish, the Scots and the Welsh much as the Germans have treated their Slav neighbours—with a mixture of ruthlessness and mockery."
—*The Observer*, Sunday, 12th March 1967.

class were an extremely aggressive, able and unscrupulous element. They were analphabetic, idle, only in the most superficial fashion Christianised: war, fighting and aggression were their favourite occupation and form of sport: at worst their constant aggressions were a sort of organised, large-scale hooliganism or gangsterism. With the Reformation came a subtle but fundamental—and to us now, familiar—change. When it was consummated—as everywhere where it took place the Reformation in England was the achievement of a Party, who enforced their will and in due course their mentality on a reluctant and indeed for a long time fiercely unwilling majority—when it was consummated the Christian religion had in effect suffered a reduction to the dimensions of a national cult: religion had become a function of nationality: the God conceived of and worshipped can be identified as no longer the Ground of all Being but a tribal Idol or national Deity whose function it was to preside over the triumphant aggression and expansion of "His" England.

The change was something more subtle than public subscription to the proposition, God is English. It concerned not so much a notion as the way itself in which the mind works, the aspect under which human realities are conceived or apprehended. (As such it is not subject to contradiction or logical disproof, since it it is not primarily an idea but a *mode* of perceiving or apprehending or reacting to reality.) Gurian, had he directed his attention to the phenomenon, would have found in this "Englishism" an even "purer" form of Bolshevism than German National Socialism, insofar as "Englishism" has been even less burdened—in fact hardly burdened at all—by an ideological structure justifying the psychological situation, the metaphysical state of the will, in notional or doctrinal terms. Very little if any ideological structure or doctrinal system was felt to be necessary to justify an attitude and state of the will whose rightness was simply felt to be "obvious"—although of course such expressions as "God's Englishman," which imply a doctrine, were quite seriously made and taken.

All the other processes, however, can be recognised as having been followed out in classical form. First the negating movement or repudiating action of the will at the immediate and sub-rationally conscious level on confrontation with the non-English "other." Followed by the strict dualisation of human reality, its categorisation into "English" and "the rest." Followed again by the attachment of all value concepts to the first of those two categories. This remains descriptive of the pre-fully-rational state of the English consciousness even today. For centuries it has been —in a strictly literal sense—*unthinkable* that such concepts as Truth, Right, Justice, Freedom, and so on, could be exclusive of or set over against the concept England or English in the mind. It could not be so because the concepts had been fused and become one. Right could never be validly conceived as contrary to "England's Right." Might could not be conceived of as in any lawful sense opposed to the Might of England. Humanity itself was not rightly and fully conceived except insofar as it meant English. Just as Freedom to the Reformation Protestant could mean only one thing, the absolute supremacy of the Kirk and the conditioning of everyone with its doctrines, to the Communist Freedom can mean nothing whatever but the establishment of Communism and the making of everyone Communist, similarly in post-Reformation England Freedom in its true or complete sense meant coming under the rule of England, being or being made English, than which no more ideal or true Freedom—and no more fortunate fate—could be conceived.

Naturally this involved struggle, and to do them credit the English accepted it as their burden and did not shrink from it. It is important not to gather the impression that there is anything in the least ironically intended about such a statement: on the contrary there has even been a peculiar sort of heroism about English acceptance of the burden of making the whole world English, a burden which must continue to weigh upon the spirit until that objective be accomplished. Nor do we speak of anything so superficial—so *conscious*—as sentiments or particular objectives at particular moments, but of something much more deep-seated, and therefore by so much the more ineradicable, of the very *mode* in which the English consciousness, down to the sub-rationally conscious, works in the context of the human reality. There can be no doubt about that "Englishman's burden" as an element in consciousness. We all recall the following lines from a "poem" which formed part of the conditioning process which was our "education"—

162

"The meteor flag of England
Shall yet terrific burn,
Till danger's troubled night depart,
And the star of peace return"

—which I quote not because of the first two lines, which are a
simple expression of the aggressive stage or element in the
complex, but for the sake of the last two, which are unintentionally
revealing as to the nature of the phenomenon in two of its
constant features. As a means of constantly rallying and retaining
popular support, a Party like that of the Reformation Protestants,
the Communists, the German National Socialists, has invariably
as part of its technique made great use of a fear which it whips
up and maintains at a high, even if necessary hysterical pitch, fear
of external enemies who are represented as constantly lying in wait
to attack and take away their "liberties." The respective populations can at any time be raised to a frenzied degree of support for
the Party regime by the threat that otherwise "the bogey-man will
get them." As Gurian put it with reference to National Socialist
Germany: *"The Jew, the emigre, the Bolshevik is the bugbear that
justifies a constant tension of all the social forces, a more intense
concentration of power (i.e.* in the Nazi Party), *a permanent frenzy
and a state of siege.* Otherwise 'he' or 'they' would again get the
upper hand."

The bugbear that has held the Protestant populations together
in a constant tension of the social forces—Scotland is a prime
example, *the* prime example—kept an intense concentration of
power in the hands of the Kirk, and maintained the people at
large in a permanent frenzy and state of siege, was of course the
bogey of "Rome." The whole people were maintained in a state
of frenzied adherence to the Kirk out of the fear that otherwise
"Rome" would come back and "get them," destroying their
Protestant "liberties"—Liberty and Protestantism having become
a fused concept. (Even to this day the Scottish element in the
population of Scotland, like so many conditioned subjects of a
Pavlovian experiment, is capable of being stampeded in any
desired direction by the simple invocation of the fear of "Rome."
Given the correct initial conditioning, one may spend half a century
in the consistent attempt to rid consciousness of all conditioned,

163

non- or anti-rational influences, and still require only to hear the word "Rome" pronounced in a certain tone, to come upon it at certain moments unawares, to experience the same apprehensive shiver, the same invasion of dark threat and shapeless fears. For it goes without saying that this "Rome" is nothing more than the trigger-word of a conditioned reflex action, and has no existence outside the consciousness, the emotions and nerves, of those who are affected by it: nothing exists objectively or in the real world to correspond to it. "Rome" is not a concept abstracted from objective reality but a state induced by a particular stimulus: but then its purpose never was to impart knowledge but to induce action, the action of frenzied adherence to the Kirk, the Party in absolute control.)

Similarly—and recognisable more easily as it is not something happening in ourselves—it has always been an unflagging part of Communist technique to maintain the mentality appropriate to a permanent state of siege by representing the "Communist father-land" as permanently surrounded by the "capitalist," or "bourgeois," or "colonialist"—it was even at one time the "demo-cratic"—powers, perpetually plotting to "return" and deprive the Communist populations of their "liberties"—Liberty in this case having been fused with the concept Communism.

Now we are in a position to understand in its context the con-cept of "danger's troubled night" in the quoted poem. In the case of England the threat came quite simply from "the foreigners"— ontologically, the non-English "other"—who were conceived of and *felt* to be continuously plotting darkly to attack England and take away the "liberties" of the English. It was of no consequence that those liberties in the case of the great body of Englishmen were illusory, never more so than under the "glories" of the age of industrial development and expansion, when from generation to generation the working population of England existed in condi-tions of virtual slavery, disfranchised of the most meagre conditions of personal independence and self-respect. It did not matter because there had been a familiar fusion of concepts so that liberty meant in effect not liberty but, simply, being English. It was this liberty, or liberty in this conceptual transformation, that was felt as constantly threatened by "the foreigners," whose slightest activity even in their own legitimate interests constituted the "knavish tricks" which the National Anthem confidently calls on God to frustrate and confound: that being His proper function, since He has in effect been reduced to the concept and status of a tribal or national deity, whose true providence is to sanction and promote English policy and ensure their success in war.

The second element in the phenomenon follows naturally—the part represented by the conception of the "return" of the "star of peace." Peace is another concept which suffers transformation in the case of all those aggressive dualisms springing from an initial Nay-say. To the Protestant Peace meant exclusively, and could have no meaning apart from, the triumph of the Kirk: that is why they would not accept toleration even when it was offered them; it would have been a betrayal, a stopping short of the establishment of true Peace, Liberty, etc. To the Communist Peace, true or ideal Peace, is inconceivable short of the universal triumph of Communism: anything less is a halting by the way, at best a tactic forced on them by circumstances they are not yet able to overcome. Similarly, to the English, Peace could have no ideal meaning that excluded the conception of the supremacy of England; peace without the defeat of the foreigner was inconceivable. In the case of the English, Peace ultimately meant exactly what it meant Gurian's definition of it in the case of German National Socialism —*"the supremacy of the best race and the best nation."*

The present situation in the world at large no longer permits the active, aggressive stage of this national "English" complex. Nevertheless the earlier stages—the primary negation of the "other," justified by the radical dualisation of reality as it comes to comprehension in the mind, with the transformation of concepts and the attachment of positive emotional elements to *one* of the categories, all proceeding below the level of full consciousness —still remain universally characteristic of the English soul. (This explains among many other things how it is possible for numbers of Englishmen of personally kindly disposition—personal disposition is irrelevant in this context, which concerns *the mode of conceiving reality*—numbers, to take an example, of persons who have given years of devoted, disinterested public service in distant, once-subject countries—are continuously at once puzzled and hurt at the universal detestation in which their nation is apparently held. The fact is that what is unconscious or sub-rationally conscious in themselves is at once apprehended by everyone else, and nothing is more unacceptable, indeed intolerable to non-English "others" than to be aware that their place has been fixed in an inescapably inferior category by someone—however personally kindly—who cannot help but "know" himself as "Chosen" and superior.) However the changes in the world have of necessity brought about the suspension of the aggressive stage in the English complex, it is still the case that the least-endowed sort of Englishman continues to "know" that something in him, his being English, in fact, renders him *in an absolute way* superior to one of any other nation, were it Leonardo da Vinci—(no one denies that foreigners are clever; it has been one of their most detestable if incomprehensible features: but it is a characteristic they share with devils and monkeys.) The attitude is, as it has been for centuries, in the English air. It begins to form with the first breath of consciousness. Before the Psychology Section of the British Association at its meeting in 1965 the findings were given of a survey of young English children before they had reached the stage of gathering the most basic information about other countries. In the words of the psychologist who had conducted the survey: "The term 'English' was for English children associated with a positive emotional tone. One might say that 'English' is equivalent for them to 'nice,' and 'not English' to 'not nice' "—a first attitude which every influence in their lives will only thereafter confirm and make unconscious and ineradicable.

But although the new distribution of forces in the world no longer makes it possible for England to debouch on the field of history at the aggressive stage of the national personality complex, it has to be remembered that there were centuries on end when this was not only possible but actually a main feature of the world scene. The meteor flag of England burned terrifically all right, and all over the place.

Naturally it has been the invariable custom to present this last as if it had been the effect of purely rational and even idealistic motives. All the generations have grown up instructed that this, that or the other episode of aggression was brought about for such and such a *reason,* if not indeed in pursuit of such and such an *ideal.* But such a presentation is as unreal as it ought by now to be out of date. We have no excuse nowadays for not knowing and taking into account the fact that the great mass of human motivation, group as well as personal, is sub-rational in origin, in the area from which it derives its "drive," and that the "reasons" and far more the 'ideals" are imported after the primary and causal event, provided, that is, by the part of the mind whose function it is to make men's actions appear rational, capable of being comprehended not to say approved in the upper or rationally conscious areas of the mind. (I think we have already mentioned the Frenchman's remark that man was given speech to conceal his thoughts; and stated on our own account that it would be even truer to say that *man was given thought to conceal his motives,* even from himself, particularly from himself. And it is in the light of this fact that history calls out to be rewritten.) From this point of view the history of England as we have had it presented to us from our earliest years betrays itself as a sort of fairy story designed to disguise, mask and make acceptable a very different, less "edifying" but truer tale.

Nor will it entirely do, though it be truer, to say, as one has heard it said, that basically "the policy of England from start to finish has never had any other objective than the material aggrandisement of England." Such an interpretation still leaves out of account the primary motivation pressing up from below the rational area of consciousness, the *will* in the initial Nay-say working through the dualisation of reality in the manner we have seen, and felt in the spirit like a burden—the pressure of the non-English "other" which could only be resolved or removed when the whole of reality had been compelled to assimilate itself to the objective which was contained as its implied "end" in that initial will—as it were, until the God the whole world worshipped was the English national Deity and of English nationality. Behind the "reasons" always given for English policy, still farther behind the alleged "ideals," co-present with the stimulus of the motive of avarice, was the essential, pre-rational, settled and constant impulse to compel the outer reality to accept assimilation to the English will to be disembarrassed of the "other."

(Space would not permit us to endeavour to demonstrate the presence of the negating will working through the conceptual dualisation of human reality throughout the whole period of English post-Reformation history. One imagines it could be fairly

167

easily shown at work, for instance, in the Cromwellians, who in their dealing or confrontation with non-English "others" were doubly apportioned a "Chosen" status and condition, first in being English and second in being "Saints." It would be naive to suppose that towards the Scottish and Irish nations the pre-rational will of the Cromwellians contained as its ordained "end" or objective anything short of their final genocide: what was lacking was not the will but the technical means. The latter, such as bomb-power and the gas chamber had not been invented, and there were physical limits to the slaughter of human beings that could be achieved by hand; exhaustion eventually set in. Historically the English were by nature a very cruel people, not least to each other—a review some time ago (in *The Times Literary Supplement*) of a sociological study of the industrial age opened with the words: "The English are the cruellest race in history to their own children," and not so long ago, historically speaking, the savagery of their penal laws—the "Bloody Code"—was a bye-word—nevertheless one is not, I think, wrong in detecting in the behaviour of the Cromwellians in Scotland, as in Ireland, something which was not merely temperamental, or emotional and of the moment, but indicative of the presence in the mind of a dual category which was ontological in character, from the roots of the conception of *being*. In other words the confines of the concept of "Scots" or "Irish" did not touch in the minds of the Cromwellians the limits of their concept of "humanity."

An example nearer both in time and to recollection would be the behaviour of the victors towards their prisoners and the general civil population following the Battle of Culloden. The contemporary accounts attest the presence in the mind of an element *different from* mere temperamental cruelty unleashed: we cannot help but feel ourselves in the presence of *a negation of a "kind" of human beings* down to the roots of their humanity itself. The Scots who helped the English, and were little behind them in ferocity, were Calvinists, and consequently provided with their own particular "built-in" ontological negation and radically dualised apprehension of human reality. *The Gael were at that time in actual fact in their consciousness the people of highest general culture in Europe. Nevertheless to both the English and their Scottish Calvinist allies they were outside the confines of think-*

able true humanity: neither set of men was able to "think" the Gael and simultaneously entertain in the mind the concept of "full humanity.")

The scrutiny of history with such facts about the pre-rationally conscious mind in view could be fruitfully carried very far afield.

It might be directed to such an event as the French Revolution, for instance—it was not for instance *tout simple* an affair of starving peasants—starving peasants don't make revolutions; and in any case it was not the peasant who was liberated by the Revolution but the bourgeois, and the bourgeois is by definition a negator. (But in general successful Revolutions have represented the triumph of negator elements, Nay-sayers to the non-"I": when their dust has settled the same figure has always crawled out of the debris, the figure of the bourgeois.) Insofar however as *ideas* were involved in the French Revolution, those ideas can be seen as having formed precisely such a protective shield over the mind, or rather the unconscious will, of the Revolutionary Frenchman as was formed over the Reformation Protestant by his theology, as illustrated on page 123. The French intellect with all its virtues has a weakness for a rather shallow or facile sort of rationalising, and it was this at the Revolution which achieved the ascendancy over the higher function of the mind, which is the apprehension of Reality. One might say without over-simplification that while the Reformation represented the assertion of the primacy of the Will over the Intellect by the means of theological formulations, the French Revolution equally liberated the sub-rationally-conscious Will by means of the assertion of the primacy of the Reason over the Intellect.

When I speak of rationalism here, I mean specifically the standpoint (conscious or unconscious) that only that is true, only that is *real,* which is capable of being contained within our ideas, and moreover that it is true, or real, only to the extent and in the manner in which it exists in us in the form of our ideas, or in other words that *our ideas exhaust Reality.* To adopt such a position is to be liberated at one stroke from all that transcends our ability to translate it into ideas. *Mutatis mutandis,* allowing for the difference of time, place and person, the thinkers of the French Revolution and those who followed or were influenced by them, reached by means of their philosophical rationalism an identical position with that which the Reformers and their followers reached by means of their theology, *that of being free of the obligation of obeisance to all reality beyond their apprehensions* or capable of being translated into or contained in their ideas, freedom from all inapprehensible, therefore overshadowing, and consequently unacceptable reality not-the-self.

The fact that God was invoked by both the Reformers and the French Revolutionists involved no contradiction, since the God invoked was conceived in both cases as the projection of their inner state and had no function except that of being the Supreme Guarantor of the rightness of their opinions.

In both cases, similarly, as in all other such cases, the intoxicating sense of liberation resulting (at any rate at first) from the implicit repudiation of the "not-the-self" was confused with and illicitly taken for proof of the truth of the ideas or doctrines that were merely its rationalised justification.

It is important not to gain the impression that we are to regard the present state of the West as the product solely of influences descended from and interior formations associated with the events we have particularised, Communism, the Reformation, etc., etc. In endeavouring to assess the ancestry or parvenance of the "mind" of a culture—and in proportion as it is a developed culture with complex strands of influence—we cannot ignore for instance the element of speculative thought, of philosophy. There is a widespread notion that philosophy is an abstruse subject which concerns only philosophers and has no bearing on life, the life of ordinary men as it is lived from day to day "in the street." Nothing could be farther from the truth. The fact is that the ordinary man, without being aware of it, lives also by philosophy of one brand or another, which can constantly be detected by those skilled in the science secreted like an implication in his day-to-day speech. Such are philosophies which have not only had sufficient vitality in themselves but have also and simultaneously answered sufficiently to pre-rational needs and subconscious impulses-of-seeking in the will, on leaving the philosopher's study to make themselves at home—deprived of course of their academic dress and technical vocabulary—in the market-place, the counting-house and the con-

170

ference of statesmen; this, of course, while the great mass of the persons concerned have never heard the name of the philosopher in question, or if they have do not associate it with the notions and opinions they glibly and confidently pronounce and which they suppose to be their own and to have occurred to themselves as an explanation of this or that element of life or aspect of experience.

In this connection one cannot omit mention of the father of modern philosophy, from whom subsequent speculative thought derives its paternity by one line of descent or another, namely Descartes. It is undisputed that this seventeenth century Frenchman stands philosophically, and more than philosophically, at the very door of the modern age. What will immediately now alert our attention—one might say arouse our suspicion—is the fact that his is a philosophy of strict dualism—and we may well regard this as a measure of his wrongness from the outset, for as we have seen the dual category is an element contributed by the mind—one might say by the weakness of the mind—to any act of understanding, and falsifies reality "not-the-self" by at once dividing its unity and reducing its complexity.

For Descartes man was not *one*, possessing the integrity of a single whole, but a dual being, a spirit seated in a body, "an angel driving a machine." Furthermore, whereas in pre-Cartesian philosophy truth, regarded as the correspondence of the mind with the object, had been seen as the achievement of the Intellect working always upon the data supplied by the Senses, the achievement of Descartes was to separate the parts of the Senses and the Intellect in the formation of knowledge—and not all the ingenuity of subsequent philosophers succeeded in reuniting them. Descartes introduced a vital cleavage between mind and matter, soul and body, spirit and nature, and that being so all subsequent philosophies insofar as they descended from his, inevitably by way of action and reaction erred by the exaggeration of one or the other, either the exaltation of reason at the expense of the senses, or of the world of the tangible to the disparagement of the world of the spirit.

It would require a book in itself, and a large one, to show how Cartesianism and the philosophies that followed after and derived from it seeped down to the generality because they met this or that pre-rational and subconscious movement-of-seeking in the will, and how those philosophies though not known to be philosophies provided and do provide the rational justification for in varying degree unconsciously desired courses of action, and so have played their part in the formation of the modern world. I may however quote, on the ground of possible usefulness, the following paragraphs from what I wrote many years ago on the subject of the Final Effects of the Cartesian Revolution—(it being always understood meantime that I do not of course subscribe to the notion that philosophy is, or necessarily must be, merely an elaborate projection of or answer to subjective, pre-rational need. On the contrary, philosophy, when it is itself, can and ought to be a free, rational activity engaged in in the disinterested pursuit of truth for its own sake and irrespective of the personal dispositions of the philosopher. In other words philosophy in itself is not a particular manifestation of psychology or projection of a soul-condition, but the disinterested attempt of the Intellect to conform itself upon Reality specifically as regards Ends.)

I said: "Perhaps we are now in a position to begin to estimate the effects of the Cartesian revolution in other and more diffuse spheres than the philosopher's study. It was stated that it is the thoughts of philosophers, divested of their technical dress and finding their way down to the man in the street in the simplified or even crude form in which his mind is able to grasp them, which to a large extent determine the outlook or mental climate of an age. If it be true, then, that the ordinary person thinks as he does largely because the philosophers of a previous age thought as they did, what ideas which in some form or other are widely held today are the products of the line of philosophic speculation initiated by Descartes, and what have been their effects for good or ill on the individuals who hold them or the societies within which they have become prevalent?

"We have, in fact, seen those ideas already. We have seen, for instance, that the line of thought called subjective idealism, with its associated attitude of empiricism—as it worked out to its logical end in the system of the Scottish philosopher, David Hume— issued in an attitude of *scepticism* or *agnosticism* in regard to the existence of God, the ultimately spiritual nature of the universe, and spiritual matters generally. If, therefore, scepticism and agnosticism describe a temper of mind which is widely diffused throughout Western society today, here is one fount from which it springs. . . .

"But if Western man is much characterised today by scepticism and agnosticism in spiritual matters, and exhibits in his life the instability and lack of purpose, the loss of *vision* and the social devitalisation which result from such an attitude, there is yet one class of facts about which he suffers from no such uncertainty. Those are the facts known in popular language as 'scientific.' It is characteristic of modern man that whether or not he believes in God he certainly believes in something called Science. Here is the attitude of the empiricist. Empiricism among the philosophers, therefore, resulted in the cult of 'Science' among the generality, scientists and ordinary men alike. It is of the cult of 'Science' to hold and to assert that the hard, brute facts with which science is concerned are the *only* facts, that the truths established by science are the whole of truth, and that in consequence knowledge of a spiritual kind is unreal knowledge, or in other words that spiritual realities are not in fact realities at all but simply projections of our own mental and emotional states. Such an attitude in fact became very widespread in modern times and has done incalculable harm to the development of the spiritual side of man, not only where religion is concerned but also in the whole area of aesthetic expression and appreciation. For it amounted to the worship of Science, the elevation of Science to the place from which scepticism had ousted God. But science is the creation of the mind of man, and it is not in the nature of the human mind to find satisfaction in the worship of its own creature; the knowledge of material things is no substitute for the knowledge of God. Thus the belief in Science was doomed in the long run to end in disillusionment; and in actual fact a growing disillusionment with this substitute-religion is contributing in no small degree to the present unsettlement and bewilderment of men's minds, for many in recent times had no other faith.

"Closely connected with the cult of Science, and derived from the same source, is the worship of mechanism and the merely material which has been so marked a feature of recent and modern times. The realities with which science puts us in touch belong to the quantitative order, and such an over-concentration upon those realities as has characterised recent centuries could only result in an obsession with quantity to the neglect of quality. The things that impress our contemporaries are those that concern size, speed, and the like, not those that concern the *qualities,* moral, aesthetic, intellectual. Thus the influence of Cartesian thought was to lead by a straight course to that exclusive direction of the Western mind towards matter which has culminated in a condition of affairs in which the spirit seems about to be stifled altogeher.

"Even more far-reaching and more disastrous than the effects of any specific doctrine deriving from Descartes's thought, has been the influence of his *spirit.* Cartesian thought, as we have seen, was dominated throughout by a fundamental *dualism.* Neither the external universe nor man himself was a unity. Matter and spirit were conceived as opposed and irreconcilable principles, as were soul and body in man himself. Now once such an attitude became established in the mind it was inevitable that it should affect or colour the total mental outlook; so that men's thinking about matters far other than those which form the specific subject-matter of philosophy would be unconsciously dualistic. When it came to affect men's thinking about social life and social activities, this dualism introduced, or re-introduced, by Descartes was productive of the most momentous changes. For it meant that the political and economic activities of society (*i.e.* those corresponding to *matter* in the philosophical system) tended to be regarded henceforward as unrelated to the spiritual side of social activity, *i.e.* morality, the arts, religion. In other words, politics, economics, the operations of finance, were freed from ethical restraints and began to be pursued as if they possessed ends of their own which were superior, or at least indifferent, to the ends of society and the general good of man. Such a development could only be—and has been—productive of great harm to the spiritual side of man's nature. Coming at the time when the great advance in scientific knowledge was about to make man the undisputed master of the physical universe, it meant that the great advance in Industrialism was carried out in a spirit of the most ruthless disregard of ethical considerations, and the results were soon to be seen in the appalling conditions, of housing and the like, and in the widespread social evils, which it brought into existence. A passage from the French contemporary philosopher, Maritain, is worth quoting on the point. He says—'In such a conception (Cartesian dualism

174

transferred into the order of political and economic relations) politics and economics have each their own peculiar and specific ends, which are not human ends, but purely material ends. The end of politics is the material prosperity, the power and success of the State, and everything that may procure such an end—even an act of treachery or an act of injustice—is *politically* good. The end of economics is the acquisition and limitless increase of riches, material riches as such. And anything that may procure such an end—even an act of injustice, even oppressive and inhuman conditions of life—is *economically* good. Justice, friendship, and every truly human value thenceforth become alien to the structure of political and economic life as such, and if morality intervenes with its peculiar exigencies, it will be to engage in conflict with political and economic reality, with political and economic science. An "economic man" will be invented whose sole function is to accumulate material goods. If you attempt to duplicate him with a man subject to the control of morality, a truly human man, the duplication will be ineffective; the economic man, whose appetite is insatiable, will in reality eat up the moral duplication and everything else, and exert himself to pound, like an ogreish machine, the wretched true humanity toiling in the basements of history.' He ends—'This kind of political and economic physics has really poisoned modern culture.'

"We see, therefore, that if modern man is sceptical in religious matters, and unhappy because of it, if he is bound to disillusionment as an adherent of the cult of 'Science,' if he is suffering from the effects of an Industrial System built up on the assumption that ethical considerations are foreign to the world of economic activity, if he has been a witness or himself a victim of devastations and social chaos and destruction resulting from conflicts among nations which themselves resulted from the pursuit of political ends as if they were independent of human ends; then a part, and a not inconsiderable part, of the responsibility for such a state of affairs rests with the type of thinking whose introduction is called in philosophy the Cartesian Revolution."

(It should be pointed out of course that all such results were very far from the intention or expectation of Descartes himself, who was a human and indeed a religious man.)

It will be appreciated of course that when I was writing the above I had a different formal object in view; I was approaching the subject of actual philosophies primarily and specifically with the object of elucidating the ideas involved, *i.e.* as ideas. Whereas in this book we have been trying to work down to the identification of pre-rational and pre-ideological situations in the personality with a view to showing how they were causally related to the sort of ideas they were attracted to or "picked up," and the kind of action that resulted. We should have little difficulty however in reading the quoted paragraphs from our own point of view. We can easily see, for instance, how *any* dualistic system of ideas will recommend itself on sight through the relief it offers from the burden of the complexity of reality and the easy access it affords to the pleasure of a sense of knowledge. As to "Science," we all have the experience any day of hearing persons with no more real knowledge of science than a sheep, saying "Science says" in preface to a declaration of their own uninstructed opinion. In other words "Science" among the generality has simply been elevated to the position of "God" among the sectaries, as the Supreme Guarantor of private opinion and Supreme Justificator of personally desired courses of action. Similarly it is not difficult to see that the notion that politics and economics have their own ends, which are not general human ends, would at once be perceived as "true" by those who were already unconsciously possessed of the impulse to pursue those ends in the spirit of disembarrassment of ethical as of theological restraints.

Anyhow, what we wanted to show was that philosophical speculation has been yet another route along which the world and in particular Western humanity has travelled to its present state : we wanted to make the particular point that, given the circumstances and occasion, philosophical notions can equally with theological formulations appear to possess an "obvious" "truth" insofar as they may be equally fitted to rationalise a movement of ego-aggression against the non-"I" at the ontological level of primary motivation. In other words, philosophical notions, as in the French Revolution and Descartes, equally with theological formulations as at the Reformation, can be fitted to function as the Mask.

In sum, the real, the ultimate, determinant question about any character in history (as in day-to-day living) is not what he did (although that has its importance), or what he said, or what he thought (or even what he thought he thought) but *what was the real state of his will.*

Burnes, sound as ever, was aiming in this direction when he opined, "The hert's aye the pairt aye that maks us richt or wrang."

IV

I HOPE we have now seen that each of those episodes which
have continually recurred throughout history—the multitudinous
forms of Gnosticism, Manichaeism, the Reformation, the French
Revolution with its "rational" "mind," "Englishism," Communism,
German National Socialism, etc., with their ideology or doctrine-
system—was, in its deepest essence, in effect THE BRANDISH-
ING OF A CLENCHED FIST IN THE FACE OF
APPREHENDED BUT REPELLED OR REPUDIATED
REALITY; reality repelled, negated or rejected because apprehended at the first or instantaneous level as constricting, dwarfing
or overshadowing the *being*, "I." (Assuming its technical possibility the dust-wrapper of this book really ought to show—at first
sight a startling conception and conjunction—such easily recognisable figures as King Henry VIII, John Knox, Adolf Hitler and, let
us say, Khruschev standing brotherly-wise shoulder to shoulder,
each displaying the sign of the clenched fist, while behind them
stretch an innumerable multitude of faceless heads and clenched
fists, with banners here and there held aloft bearing such designa-
tions as Albigenses, Cathari, Kudugers, Patarenes, Bogomils,
Bulgars and so on all the way to, far in the distance, Manichees
and Gnostics.) Each of these movements in other words represents—and this is what makes it what it really *is*—an ego-aggressive
(and therefore of course anarchic) movement within the total
universe of *being*, an aggression of the ego as such into the area of
"other" reality, an annihilation-by-intent—at the metaphysical
level of the will—of *being*, not-"I." In every case the joy of
liberation which the conviction first arouses, and which is enormously, even in certain individuals and periods deliriously
augmented by it, is the joy of a spirit *because the universe of
being has been contracted to the proportion of its own limitation*,
such a contraction having been the unavowed and in varying degree
unconscious object of the whole occasion.

In other words every one of those movements so numerous
throughout history (as equally in contemporary society) which has
advanced itself on the social plane by the action of a membership
of "illuminates" or "Chosen" persons, represents the rationalisa-

tion passing into action of a universal human impulse, one which infests the will of every one of us and all the time:—the impulse, namely, to say Nay to the *being,* not-"I," to negate the "other." This impulse is continually being activated at the primary, pre-rationally-conscious level, on confrontation with an "other" who, either in his personal being or in his works, occasions a reaction in us as to something overshadowing, constricting or diminishing. Our reactive impulse is to repel, reject or deny such an "other," so that when this impulse has passed through the rational or idea-forming area it emerges as a judgment, as criticism, slander, denigration. Such are the "reasons" which the will collects in the idea-forming area on its way from the (negating) impulse to the plane of (hostile) acts. Of such are in large measure our judgments of others. As we saw at the beginning of this book any "other" is ultimately unknowable, so that our estimates of others can never as a rule be more than approximations or working assessments: they have no more than a working or utility value on a base of probability or partial knowledge—often not even that. And as a matter of fact what we mostly "know" of another is little more than the ideas we have ourselves formed, and we have formed them to fit the movement of the will the person or *being* concerned stimulates in us.

It goes without saying that in the act of criticising, censuring or denigrating an "other," his being or acts or works, actual or imputed, one is translated into a status or condition of superiority in his regard, "knows" oneself as "good" in comparison with his "bad." "Knowing" oneself as "good" is an end-product of the act of negation, and in any age those who are consciously "good" and regarded in their society as "the good" are in general if not indeed exclusively, simply the negators, Nay-sayers to "others" whether directly in their *being* or in their acts or endowments. In other words "the good" in their own and in general regard in any age and society are in that status by dint of being ego-aggressors into the sphere of "other" being.

So far is such an idea from being original that it happens to be the central concept of the Christian religion—I am excluding of course Reformation forms from that category and all that descended from them, *i.e.* insofar as it descended from them, for the reasons above shown, that their Christian terminology was no

179

more than a Mask to conceal their real Face from a religion-preoccupied sixteenth century. Anyone not searching for justification of an already held opinion or prior impulse but reading what the New Testament really and quite simply says can verify that Christ said again and again, even to indignation—that in fact He as it were came on earth on purpose to say—that while "the bad" as contemporarily regarded were not necessarily always the good, *"the good" as so regarded and so regarding themselves were always in God's sight the bad.* In other words, the Christian revelation was to the effect that ego-aggression into the sphere of "other" *being,* Nay-saying to the *being,* not-"I," was anarchical in the universe of *being* and therefore, to use a theological term, of the essence of Sin. There is not an instance in the whole of the Christian Scriptures where Charity, which comprises the whole of the Christian matter, cannot be rendered directly as Yea-say and Sin in some respect or another as Nay-say—*non serviam,* I will not serve; the war-cry of the rebellious angels.

Moreover, the central event of Christianity, the Crucifixion, illustrates to the uttermost the movement of the will at the metaphysical level, that is, in confrontation with "other" *being,* which we have disclosed as hidden not only behind critical and hostile judgments of other persons, and actions in their regard, but, enclosed in an apparatus of ideas, a mask of theory or of doctrine, being active and making itself felt and effective in society and on the plane of history. The fact stated to have been known to Pontius Pilate—"He knew that for envy (*i.e.* from Nay-say) they had delivered him"—strips the occasion of the Crucifixion of every pretence of having resulted from judgments originating in the sphere of objective ideas. The Crucifixion of Christ—and this manifestly holds Whoever He was—because it shows as its whole meaning the entry into history of an element of motivation at the purely primary or metaphysical level (a Nay-saying reaction on confrontation with "other" *being* before becoming fully rationally conscious—*"They know not what they do"*) explodes or blows up completely all theories or doctrines according to which History is "determined" or pre-ordained or guided by any Force or Agent or Third Party (however conceived) outside man himself. The Crucifixion, standing at the centre of history, illustrates once and for all and in the clearest possible light the fact we earlier arrived at, that *history is made by man and only by man,* acted upon at every moment by whatever is in fact acting upon or motivating him. Every contrary or alternative view of history—which means more or less every view of it which is or has heretofore been current, certainly every "philosophy of History"—is false, subjective and superstitious. In particular the assumption "built in" for centuries in the Western consciousness and still in possession of it, that history is under some "necessity" of moving "forward"—"Progress," and "the winning side is always right." Including even—or even particularly—the supposedly Christian concept of Divine Providence ruling History, playing an inescapable guiding role. Divine Providence can be rightly conceived as acting upon men: to regard it as acting directly on History in despite of man, moulding History according to some Plan uncomprehended by the participants but which they are nevertheless unknown to themselves compelled to act out, is pure superstition.

THE ONLY MEANS BY WHICH HUMAN SOCIETY CAN BE "CURED" OR HISTORY SALVAGED IS IN THE INDIVIDUAL HUMAN BEING, IN EVERY *BEING,* "I," BY THE RECTIFICATION OF THE ACTION OF THE WILL AT THE METAPHYSICAL LEVEL, THE SUBSTITUTION OF "YEA" FOR "NAY," THE STEADY MAINTENANCE OF "YEA" AND NOT "NAY" IN CONFRONTATION WITH *BEING,* NOT-"I."

Finally . . . the implications of the movement of Nay-say or Yea-say in the will are clear.

The point has been made already—and not by any means for the first time by me—that *whoever affirms the not-the-self by the same act and automatically affirms the self; conversely whoever affirms the self automatically and by the same act affirms the not-the-self.* Contrariwise, *whoever negates the not-the-self by the same act negates the self; and conversely whoever negates the self automatically and in the same act negates the not-the-self.* That is, by the act of Yea-say or affirmation the self becomes more *real* by the enrichment or so to speak inclusion in it of that *being,* not-the-self, which is affirmed; such a self becomes more and more a person, an autonomous *being,* spiritual in essence, fitted for the interpenetration of all that *is,* including in the ultimate *Being* itself,

181

its Ground and Origin and Essence. Contrariwise, by the act of negation or disaffirmation the self becomes less *real,* through the loss of interpenetration or augmentation by the *being* of the disaffirmed not-the-self. That is, in proportion to his negation the negator becomes less and less a *person,* more and more a mere *individual,* that is, a fragment of matter subject to passions.

(To speak Christian-wise, the act of Yea-say, of affirmation, is that act of virtue, the "good act," saving and sanctifying, which the action of Grace in us enables us to perform, while the act of Nay-say, of negation or disaffirmation, is that act to which we are prone by the non-serving tendency in us, the presence of Sin. The self by the act of Yea-say or affirmation mounts to heaven—the Peace (which is the Knowledge) of God was to be attained by men of "good," that is, affirming, *will;* and contrariwise by the act of Nay-say or negation the self reduces itself to the state of Loss, or hell.)

It is thus easy to see how the affirmation of the not-the-self through the augmentation of affirmed *being* must lead quite simply to a greater *reality* in the person or the society or period of history. *And contrariwise how negation must equally necessarily lead only to the clashing together of disaffirming units emptied of being.*

As witness the last few centuries.

Part Three

The Valve

IN SCOTLAND the triumph of the sixteenth century Party incarnating the Nay-saying impulse was all but absolutely complete. *So much so that Scotland thereafter was like a laboratory in which the experiment was conducted of impregnating a whole society with the Nay-saying pattern of motivation in all but "pure" conditions.* The control of the Party was so absolute, so unchallenged, so universally applied, so all but completely freed from the slightest organic survival of life incarnating an opposed or alternative view or movement of the will, that the *real* history, the history in essence, of the human society that was the Scottish nation from the Reformation onwards is and could not have been other than the history of the working out of the *will* as conditioned, set and directed by the Reformation Party and its agencies, the progressive leavening of the social lump by the motivation of ego-aggressive Nay-say. The "History" we have been given in the past has been a mere enumeration and discussion of *effects*—as, of political or economic events, treated as if those belonged to a closed order, of "politics" or "economics," and were the actions of an abstraction of "political man" or "economic man." Where we have been given a religious "History" of Scotland since the Reformation this has been treated as if "religion" too were a closed order, the scene of action of another abstraction of "theological man" or man conceived and considered simply as a being who holds systems of belief, a being whose nature is to be an adherent of theological formulations. It is as if for some four hundred years we had been given endless descriptions about a pattern of symptoms in isolation from their *cause*—as for instance constant disputations about the number and distribution or pattern of skin pustules without reference to the blood condition that produced them. Alternatively it is as if the *sense* of the passage had been ignored and we have been asked to be satisfied with an account of its punctuation as a true account of the passage.

HISTORY DOES NOT BEGIN TO BE WRITTEN UNTIL ALL ABSTRACTIONS OF "POLITICAL MAN" OR "ECONOMIC MAN" OR "THEOLOGICAL MAN" ARE DISCARDED AND IT IS SEEN THAT THE CAUSE OF HISTORY IS SIMPLY MAN, MAN HIMSELF, AS HE IS IN HIS ACTUALITY.

It was this actual man, or whole man, or man himself simply as he is, who was to have impressed on him—will and ideas and motivation—the Reformation *mark*. In effect, through the universal and unchallenged ascendancy and activity of the One-Party, the Kirk (not forgetting its ancillary agency, the School) the Scots were —such was the objective—universally and from generation to generation, to be turned into "other Reformers" and their society into a society of "other Reformers," such a society as would represent the exteriorisation in social terms of the motivation of the Reformers, brought about or activated everywhere through the universal enforcement of the doctrines which were the reflection of that motivation in the rational and idea-forming area of the soul. The doctrines were to be enforced on the rational area of the mind throughout Scotland as a means of evoking everywhere in perpetuity a motion of the will identical with that which in the first instance inhabited and activated the Reformers: and so the Reformers were to perpetuate themselves for all time coming.

(*It is important to realise from the outset that there was nothing Scottish about the process, except that it was going on in Scotland, happening to the Scots, and equally that there was nothing Christian about it either except that the characteristic movement of the will having risen to the surface in the sixteenth century, of necessity made use of Christian terms in the formulation of the doctrinal structures which were its rational explanation and justification.* The concept of Necessity in human life and destiny (as in the doctrine of Predestination), the concept of a radically dualised humanity, the concept of the radical evil of human nature and even nature itself: these are not Christian. On the contrary.)

The implanting of a settled, consistent movement of Naysaying in the will of every whole man or actual man making up a community was of necessity bound to colour or as it were haunt all their consciousness thereafter and throughout every individual life—"the shadow on the rose"—and unconsciously inhabiting their motivation to have presided over all the changes their action brought about in the life of their society. Man impresses himself on his society, and brings about changes in it, by the activity of his faculties, and the dynamic or change-effecting faculty is the will: therefore *the history of a nation-society impregnated or inhabited throughout by a principal or supervening motivation of*

186

Nay-say active in its members would be bound to show as its main line the translation of the motive of Nay-say into every form of private consciousness and public action: this would be its *real* history. The error of Scottish history writing has been to ignore or overlook this fact—and even to present the actual events which marked the process as having been part of a "necessary" development representing "Progress," although as we have demonstrated both of those terms are subjective, conceptual, superstitious, loaded with illicit value judgments, and have nothing whatever to do with history.

To come to actual aspects—(and in order to begin somewhere) —we may recollect Ninian Kennedy's "aside" that the *real* reason why the Reformers destroyed the churches of their days was that they could not have built them, that is, that they would not accept, could not tolerate the evidence incarnated in their excellence that there were greater human gifts than had been conferred on *them*. The doctrine that they were "vain works of a totally reprobate human nature" was something which adhered to the primary negating impulse in its passage through the idea-forming area of the mind, whose function was to confer upon it rational justification. No Reformer or descendant of the Reformers in the order of the spirit, could have found it tolerable to sit in worship of his Deity (the Deity conceived no longer as the Ground of All Being but as the Supreme Guarantor of the rightness of the Reformers' opinions, the Justificator-in-Chief of their Nay-saying motivation), no Reformer by his spirit could have tolerated to sit in worship—in effect, in worship of his own limitations—surrounded by works which pointed up those limitations and reduced them to their true assessment by standing in witness of their paucity. Therefore the Reformation was bound to have been followed by the total cessation of the public art of architecture—of architecture, that is, *as* an art—and not only of architecture but of every "public" and therefore publicly controllable art—as for instance the drama, music of the choral or orchestral sort, the music of single instruments (as, for instance, the organ) which by their nature could not be hidden from public sight. In fact, those all ceased forthwith and on the instant. It was from a quarter of a millennium to three hundred years before the force and immediacy of the radical Nay-say in

187

public feeling and opinion had moderated, at least in the larger centres of population, sufficiently to permit a reappearance of any interest in those arts and activity in respect of them.

Even so, there is a subtle yet radical difference—in fact all the difference in the interior human world—between the attitude to art and creativity of those in later and contemporary times who are engaged in or attracted to them and the attitude which prevailed formerly, *i.e.* before the Reformation, a difference which involves the basic movement of the will at the metaphysical level. That difference consists in this, that within the total view of life the practice or appreciation of art and creativity generally is seen or "felt" as no more than something *permitted,* instead of—what it is— something *enjoined in the very nature of being.* The movement has yet gone no farther than from the *illicit* to the *permissible.* (As witness, for instance, the fact that those who teach art or music are universally regarded within the teaching profession as a sort of second-class members, concerned with what are no more than fripperies or "frills".) With such an enormous leeway as compared with Europe elsewhere, and such a radically cramping attitude haunting if not presiding over creativity today, it is no wonder— was in fact inevitable—that Scotland, four hundred years after the Reformation and as an extended though direct consequence of it, should qualify for its often awarded title of "the greatest cultural desert in Europe."

It is scarcely digressing to point out that the withholding of an affirmative motion of the will from the element of creativity was merely a particular aspect of a general withdrawal of assent from most of the activities of life. The doctrine of the radical depravity of human nature and the worthlessness of works logically shut the will off even from the sphere of ethical activity itself. *Nothing was left that was licit save the activity of functioning membership of the Kirk. That and practical or material concerns.* It did not require Calvin's injunction to his followers to get rich to ensure that the immediate and continuing consequence of the Reformation was an immersion of those seized by its spirit in the sphere of material things and activities. This—both among formal adherents of Protestant doctrine in its day and equally among their descendants who had and have forgotten the doctrine—was far more than a belief that riches are desirable in themselves. It was involved in *the aspect under which the Scots have conceived life* for the last four hundred years that material preoccupations were licit and enjoined—*real,* one might say—while the things of the creative spirit of man were at worst forbidden and at best *unreal* and barely or possibly permissible. This albeit subconscious aspect under which life is viewed remains universal among the Scots, and it descends by direct line from the Reformation.

Two things are manifest. First, that as an attitude to life it laid itself open to reinforcement by influences from the world at large such as that of Cartesian materialist dualism—(albeit the consequences of the Reformation could have produced and did produce by themselves identical effects, unaided by external influences of popularised philosophy:—*the typical monument of the pre-Reformation spirit is cathedrals, of the Reformation spirit, industrial slums.*) Second, that such a way of conceiving life was, and is, fatal to the practice of the arts in such a spirit and to such effect as would have avoided the dereliction of Scotland to the status of "the greatest cultural desert in Europe."

But there was another element in the situation, and that concerned the material on which the Reformation had to work, *the sort of humanity who were to be impressed with its spiritual typation.*

The history of the Scottish people had from the beginning been crammed with the sort of events that are of the very stuff of tragedy, of the heroic, both on the national and personal level, and with situations evocative of high emotion, therefore of the very stuff of poetry and music. With the nature of both the Scottish people were initially greatly endowed and to both exceptionally and passionately addicted. (Moreover they had always been penetratingly aware of the *reality* of *place.* One of the two greatest philosophers of mediaeval times was a Scot, and one of the crucial points on which he differed from his rival was in that he insisted on *the knowability of the individual object.* It was not perhaps surprising in one of his country of origin. In any case the physical surface of Scotland is such as exceptionally to throw up into relief even quite small natural objects—trees, houses, rocks—and of course even more summits, slopes, crags, dramatic acclivities, so that to the aware ego they can all be even startlingly real and dramatically a part of the appurtenance of perceptual and emotional life; and it was so with the Scots, the Albannaich, among whom every slope had its elegy and every burn its troubadour.) *That vast inheritance of song and poetry and private music the Reformers and their successors with their best and long-continued zeal failed to extinguish.*

Most formidable of all the obstacles to the imposition of the doctrinal formulations and even more the essence of the matter, the accompanying negating action of the will, was the Gaelic language, the language at the time of the majority of the people, more particularly as it was the vehicle of transmission of an exceptionally vital tradition and a truly immense body of oral poetry, music and song of both the popular and professional or sophisticated mode (the latter of unsurpassed complexity and a matter of intensive study—it may be worthy of note in this connection that non-Reformation Scotland seems to have been the only people to have developed, in *piobaireachd,* a major art form for an instrument of its own developing and perfecting.)

The language therefore which until the Reformation had been referred to as the *lingua materna* and regarded as the mother tongue of the nation, had as a continuing priority to give place to the English language which was introduced by the Reformers and enforced as the language of the Bible and the Kirk. Even so the original Gaelic speech is known to have continued in such regions for instance as Ayrshire and Fife until past the mid-eighteenth century, that is, for two hundred years. But at the Highland line the new influences, especially linguistically, encountered for centuries an absolute barrier. And it was now in consequence that the two-race theory and sentiment had its origins, the theory that the Scots were of two totally different races whose natural condition was to be at radical enmity. It was thanks to the influence of Reformationism that in the Scottish consciousness in the areas under its control the association Gaelic=Highlander=hated and despised (because suspected if not of Catholic belief and practice at least of a non-Protestantised and non-Protestantisable consciousness) grew up. It was only in the nineteenth century that the Nay-saying motivation really took hold within the Highlands, and then only in parts of the area, and by then it was too late for it

190

to go more than part-way towards the extirpation of the enormous traditional inheritance of culture.

These facts explain the apparent contradiction—the phenomenon which has been a source of constant astonishment and perplexity to observers of other nationalities—that Scotland is on the one hand in terms of artistic development in modern forms "the greatest cultural desert in Europe," while on the other it possesses the greatest body of popular poetry and music of outstanding excellence as well as the greatest body of transmitted oral literature in Europe—this in spite of the fact that all we have now remaining is a mere fraction of the original deposit, a proportion which can never now be ascertained having been suppressed or dissipated as a result of the action of the Nay-saying motivation induced by the Reformation, with its nihilistic attitude to culture and creativity.

Secondly . . . it is essential that it should be apprehended : — *with the Reformation the Scottish nation shrank to the Kirk, and its will to the will of the Kirk. The supremacy of the Kirk was regarded as the meaning of man's entire existence. It was the standpoint from which everything was viewed and valued.*

The welfare of the nation became identified with the supremacy and will of the Kirk, and not otherwise could it be conceived thenceforward. Politics in consequence lost its content and as an activity changed its direction and objective. Whereas in all times formerly it had been the activity which had as its proper end the welfare of the state, the nation-community as such, in the centuries following the Reformation it could have only one meaning, the means taken to secure the supremacy of the Kirk and the expression of its will. Politics in its correct definition, having as its objective *the welfare of the nation-community as such,* could only be thereafter at best an unreal activity, unfitted to be supported by the will, at worst illicit, even incomprehensible, a concept incapable of formation. It was thus possible, as Ninian Kennedy foresaw and prognosticated, for the Scottish people, under the conviction that they were still as wholeheartedly devoted to liberty as ever, actually to be deprived of their liberty as a nation altogether, while supposing themselves still to possess liberty—and even more than before since they possessed the ascendant Kirk and its doctrines, into which the concept of Liberty was now for all time assumed.

Exactly this did happen. "1560—1603—1707—*these three dates are connected together by the strictest law of cause and effect. Without the Reformation the Union of the Crowns would have been impossible, the Union of the Parliaments unthinkable.*" So said the doyen of Scottish historians, the late Hume Brown, and nobody can quarrel with his judgment. The effect of the transvaluation of values and trans-association of concepts brought about by the Reformation was in the end that the Scots, originally the most nationally-conscious and freedom-loving people in Europe, were led on to lose their national status and autonomy, to be reduced from a nation into no more than a backward province in the possession of their traditional enemy, while retaining the illusion that they were still free, and even freer than ever before, since the Protestant religion remained secure in its ascendancy. Such was the effect of the transvaluation of Liberty into, simply, Protestantism, the Kirk, with the result that politics as concerning the welfare of the nation-community as such became a no longer licit activity, its end unconceivable: "real" politics, that is, politics deserving or requiring to be supported by the Will, concerned the security and ascendancy of the Kirk.

It is necessary to recall to mind yet again that the essential, the operative thing about the Reformation was not its doctrines—that secondary and as it were accidental phenomenon—but the event it resulted from and in turn evoked in the will, the mechanism which produced it and which it in turn produced within the human personality, with the mode under which this mechanism caused life and all its activities to be conceived and evaluated. So that in a people once formed or conditioned by the Reformation the same mechanism in the consciousness and subconsciousness of the personality would continue operative long after the doctrines had ceased to evoke consent or even to be known : the doctrines might and would go but the movement of the will in the context of life, the aspect under which life was conceived, with the valuations attached to its various activities, would remain, since that was what was essential. (Such a people or community would, for instance, even when they had reached the stage of being agnostic in opinion or irreligious in outlook, continue nevertheless to be controlled in its motivation and consequently in its action by the assumption in consciousness, as inherent in its conception of life, that material considerations are most important, most *real*, in the sense of most deserving to be supported by the will. Other considerations, as for instance all that concerns the welfare of the nation-community as such, the proper subject matter of politics, would long after the abandonment of the Reformation doctrines continue to be seen or "felt" as *unreal* and questionably licit considerations, that is, as not meriting or entitled to activate a supporting movement in the will. [My own experience has in this respect been utterly typical: having been rigorously conditioned at the first under the influence of the Reformation doctrines and the Reformation spirit, I have not over a period of more than sixty years of life been able to give free scope to the creative element in my personality, or to engage in philosophic speculation, or to engage actively in what concerns the welfare of my nation-community, without the haunting of a sense like guilt, a sense that all of these are activities not permitted or at the very least unbecoming to a "Saint," a "Child of God"].)

It amounts to this: the continuing effect of the Reformation has been that every Scot—whether he adhered or adheres to any contemporary form of Protestantism or not is irrelevant—has been subject to a built-in mechanism, *a monitor in consciousness,* which automatically switches aside the will when it is directed towards anything in the area of free creativity, or at any objective having to do with the welfare of his nation-community (conceived not as a number of individuals with various material or other wants but simply *as* a nation-community) and directing it into "permissible" channels, towards "permissible" objectives, such as forms of sectarian activity and anything having a material aim.

What happens, and has been happening in the Scottish consciousness for four hundred years, may be crudely illustrated as on the next page. We may note that the faculties, the senses, sentiments, emotions being aroused activate the will affirmatively towards the objectives in the sky of aspired-towards excellences. The movement of the will automatically and by itself activates in the conditioned personality the system of negations and prohibitions induced by Reformation doctrines and left behind by them as the view or estimate of life—brings on "the shadow on the

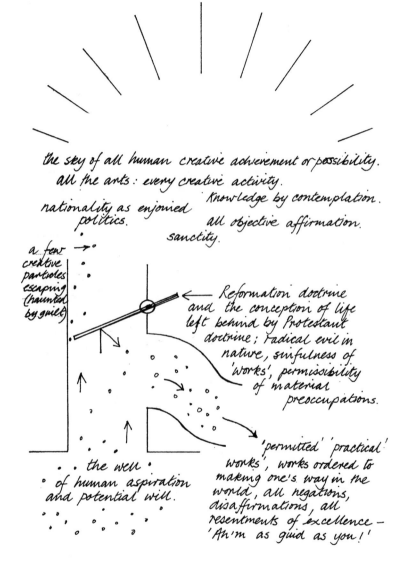

the sky of all human creative achievement or possibility.
all the arts: every creative activity.
                              knowledge by contemplation.
nationality as enjoined
       politics.   all objective affirmation.
                       sanctity.

a few →
creative
particles
escaping
(haunted
by guilt)

← Reformation doctrine
and the conception of life
left behind by Protestant
doctrine; radical evil in
nature, sinfulness of
'works', permissibility
    of material
       preoccupations.

'permitted' 'practical'
works', works ordered to
making one's way in the
world, all negations,
disaffirmations, all
resentments of excellence —
'Ah'm as guid as you!'

· · the well ·
° of human aspiration
and potential will.

rose": automatically and by the unconscious action of the will *"closes the Valve."* The way has thus been closed to affirmation of "other" being and qualitative excellence. Simultaneously and as part of the same personality event the way is left unoccluded and the will directed towards the whole range of "permitted" activities, anything negating and ego-aggressive, material aims and making one's way in the world, which can be engaged in "happily," without impediment of an induced sense of guilt, bring into the spirit the sanction of the "permitted" and are therefore clearly "good."

A particular effect of the mechanism has been far-reaching. In the fusion of concepts welded by the imputation of value judgments at the Reformation, "England" was fused to that of "Protestantism" or "the Kirk" since it was in the act identified with its triumph, a cause of its establishment as the Party in absolute power. In spite of episodes in later times when elements in Protestantised Scotland were opposed to or even at actual war with English policies of the moment, the assimilation of "England" into the compound concept of "Protestantism=Truth=Liberty, etc." remained as firmly planted as ever in the Scottish consciousness and subconsciousness. England after all was the ultimate bulwark of the Kirk and of Protestantism against the bogey of the possible recrudescence of an opposed conception of life, a revival of Yea as opposed to Nay as the dominating movement in the metaphysics of the will, the re-realisation of a state of things which would have given free play to the intellectual and creative element of human nature and consequently have reduced men of the calibre of the Reformers and their successors to the inconsiderable status of the meagrely endowed men they actually were. *Protestantism with its "liberties" was safe ultimately insofar as the country leant to England,* for which reason, to ensure the connection which made them secure in their ascendancy, *the Reformers and their successors initiated and carried out a policy of vigorous Anglicisation of the people.* They were bound by the transvaluation of values that resulted from the Reformation to be indifferent to the welfare of the Scottish nation-community *as such* because incapable of conceiving such welfare as a valid "end," the while the trans-identification of concepts caused the Anglicisation of the Scottish

195

consciousness and the leaning and even subservience of the nation to England to be indissolubly assimilated to the concept of the supremacy of the Kirk regarded as the meaning of man's entire existence. This trans-identification of concepts has had the result that right up to the present day English politics retains an association of reality and permissibility in the Scottish subconsciousness at the same time as Scottish politics, or politics concerned with the welfare of the Scottish nation-community as such, retains a status in consciousness as of something unpermitted or unreal, not licitly entitled to call up the supporting action of the will. This explains in great part why among a people still overwhelmingly Scottish in sentiment, a (Nationalist) movement which has been in the political field for the past forty years, aiming at nothing more than the resumption of autonomous national status, has had up to the present so moderate success. The great majority—although they would *like* to see such an event—are withheld from the operative step of political action in expression of their sentiment because the association continues to be active in the subconsciousness: politics as directed to the welfare of the nation-community is stultified by a sense of unreality if not impermissibility, while participation in English politics, as in the act of participating in the activity of an English party, can be performed with an unimpeded sense of participation in a *real* activity, without violation of the subconscious association of "England" with the concepts of "Liberty," "Truth," etc. as transvalued at the Reformation. *The mechanism of the Valve ensures that consciousness and aspiration towards Scottishness does not pass from the region of the sentiments to the area of the will.*

This explains another dichotomy or contradiction which has constantly baffled observers of other nationalities, the fact that the Scots can be at one and the same time conspicuously—and, by way of compensation, even aggressively—nationally-conscious and yet actively and persistently support or tolerate a political arrangement by which their nation is subdued to and submerged in England.

Thirdly . . . Ninian Kennedy, looking beyond the Reformation, said: "Farewell now to joy; this world's a dreary prison-house, with yourselves as gaolers over all men, till they be ready to be

196

damned." The effect of the Reformation and its doctrines and the valuation it placed on the elements of human life—that the works of the human spirit were worthless and sinful and the only licit activities were Kirk membership and the pursuit of material ends —was bound to be *gloom*. It could not have been otherwise in a world in which the vast majority were doomed to hell fire in any case, in spite of themselves, where life meant only passing an uncomfortable time under a spiritual tyranny while waiting to be damned. It was inevitable that gloom should have presided over the life of the Albannaich from the Reformation on, that Scotland should have become at the Reformation, what it has remained ever since, an area of human consciousness charged with gloom. Moreover, the effect of the activity of the Kirk was to act as a selecting mechanism which chose out and raised up everywhere men of the most circumscribed affirmations and most ego-aggressive impulse, "other Reformers," in other words the meanest and most envious, and elevate them to the position of tyrants in every community. Further, the Kirk and its bodies acted identically with the dictatorships of modern times, with all the appurtenance of house-visitations, inquisitions, denunciations, confiscations and so forth. All this created and maintained an atmosphere in which men of a free and would-be affirming spirit simply could not breathe. This along with (in due time) the dire effects of that other Reformation consequence, capitalist industrialism, and the loss of political freedom leading to the reduction of the nation to the condition of a neglected, backward and misgoverned province, unable to provide the opportunities and satisfactions that the life of a free community offers to its members, led vast numbers to abandon the country altogether. In my own lifetime more than two million Scots, and those of the most gifted and energetic, have emigrated —a unique phenomenon, still continuing at a constant if not increasing tempo.

One extended effect of the Reformation, therefore, has been the progressive destruction of the Scottish race in its homeland, *even biologically*.

Fourthly . . . just as I was in the act of writing this I happened to witness an episode which so exactly illustrates my next point that I give it here—a person of my acquaintance violently refusing to accept a statement—of no particular or personal consequence and having nothing to do with religion—a simple statement of a physical fact which as it happens is not only "of observation" but scientifically proved, just because for some reason which may well have been obscure to himself it was unacceptable to him, such a one getting up and going off saying with pride and arrogance, "Remember, *I'm* a Protestant!" I imagine he had no idea how perfectly he was illustrating at that moment and in that action the "freedom" "won" for us by the Reformation—"every man is entitled to think for himself": meaning, not that every man is entitled to *think* for himself (against that there could be no objection), but that every man is entitled to take what he *wills* for truth. As Ninian Kennedy foresaw, the principle of the Reformers that the will and not the intellect is and ought to be the judgment-forming faculty was soon enough taken out of their hands by those that followed and applied not to *their* (the Reformers') judgments but to their own; and as the exclusive preoccupation with religion waned the principle came to be applied not to religious opinion only but over the whole sphere of life. To oppose one's own will in opinion to others is no peculiarity of Protestants, but the Reformation gave it a sanction from religion. A Scot of the present day may well be of no religious affiliation—but every one of them, down to those of meanest intelligence and greatest resentment of others, carries about built into his consciousness a vague yet immovable conviction that at some time or other it was won for him in the past under the highest possible Sanction, won for him once and for all, that he had an absolute right to hold what opinions he pleased, in defiance of no matter how manifest objective truth—and by inference to act as he pleased on his opinions without reference to others. Such he conceives are his "Protestant liberties."

This is something far more subtle than an objective declaration that anything I choose to think is automatically true and enforcible on others—*it is unconsciously a part of the very conception of life.* It calls in the principle of voluntarism, or the primacy of the will over the intellect in matters of truth—an idea which, as a contemporary philosopher (Maritain) has pointed out, "seems inseparable in the history of philosophy from another idea, the idea of *radical evil."* (The attempt in this book has been precisely to show *why* those ideas inevitably go in company like twin ideas,

198

the reason being that both arise *necessarily* out of the same move-ment in the metaphysics of the will, the Nay-say or negating action of the personal will emerging first in the idea of radical evil because that has the function of clearing the ground for personal ego-aggression into the sphere of *being*.) In any case this principle of voluntarism or the primacy of the will, planted at the centre of the very conception of life, *turned the Scots more and more from a nation into something like a collection of hostile atoms.* It was so during centuries when the violent conflicts of sects held the field, and even when the hand of organised Reformation Protestantism relaxed its omnipresent grip the Scots were left incapable of com-bining together for any—no matter how valid—objective.

Finally . . . the principal agency apart from the Kirk whereby the effect of the Reformation continued to be imposed, equally as long as the doctrines of the Reformers were held and after they had waned in acceptance or been discarded or forgotten, and by means of which that effect—the imposition of a Nay-saying attitude over the largest area of life, the diversion of vital objectives into practical preoccupations and towards material ends, the process of Anglici-sation as a first objective—the agency by which all this continued to be rigorously imposed, was and is the system or process of Educa-tion. Whatever may be said about it from any other point of view, it is undeniable that the Scottish educational system still stands where it has always stood, clear athwart the path of any Scottish child developing in consciousness inside the traditions that are native to him, or of any who might wish to re-immerse themselves in those traditions where contact has been lost. (One recalls one's own experience—the experience of the majority of Scottish children sixty years ago—of going to school and being educated in a language which was not spoken outside school, even by the teachers.) *It is the distinction of "Scottish education," since it became universal and compulsory, to have extinguished two languages in three generations,* with of course the whole mass of associated traditions, both historical and creative-cultural, and—what was an absolute value—the unique mode of consciousness that went with them and out of which they had arisen. All other considerations aside, it is indisputable that Scottish education regards itself as successful, as having fulfilled its objective, in proportion as each generation is less Scottish than the last, in language, knowledge, culture and consciousness.

It is in such a context, such a situation, that one can perceive the purpose of the suppression of all knowledge of the Keltic past and of the Keltic rôle in history, the reason why the drama of the history of Europe is presented with one of the principal parts cut out. The Keltic past is rigorously excluded, absolutely shut off from knowledge as if it had never been, not because it was not excellent in itself and important in its rôle, but because knowledge of it might lead to identification with it, thus jeopardising the main educational aim of Anglicisation at all costs and in the shortest space of time. In pursuit of which, at the same time as the Keltic part is cut out, another character is blown up beyond all realistic historical dimensions: England is unvaryingly presented before the opening consciousness as a sort of inflated Gulliver figure treading the Lilliput of everybody else's earth. English history is universally taught—it would be truer to say imposed—in Scottish schools as if it represented history itself, real history, whereas Scottish history is taught—in the event of its being taught at all, which is by no means to be taken for granted—as if it represented something peripheral to the historical process, outside the stream of real history, non-significant. The effect is inevitably to produce a slavish and sycophantic attitude to England and everything English and an attitude varying from condescending tolerance to overt contempt—at best of regretful rejection—of Scotland and everything Scottish. In short, the historical views and judgments, along with the highly selected items of fact, inculcated in Scottish schools as history, have only the most tenuous connection with history as it was: but then the true (if unavowed and unconscious) inner purpose of the process was never to produce true historical judgments but to act as a conditioning technique or mechanism designed to produce a desired type or state of consciousness, a particular area of receptivity for required ideas, a trigger-occasion for the "right" movement of the will.

Moreover, even if a portion of the data of actual Scottish history is included in the knowledge handed down in Scottish schools, it is still the case that the method of its presentation is such as to inculcate every one of the views and notions about history that were examined and found invalid in the earlier part of this book. That is, it causes life to be conceived under the aspect of "Progress," imposes the notion that the winning side was always right, and that all that has happened since the Reformation, the triumph of Protestantism, the immersion in material ends with the consequent devastations of avarice and industrialism, universal Anglicisation, the loss of political freedom, the destruction of the native language and culture and reduction of its characteristic mode of consciousness, the incessant involvement in English wars with the systematic decimation of Scottish manhood in every generation as in a sort of abattoir, the gigantic emigrations of Scots and scarcely less gigantic immigrations of non-Scots, all leading in the end to *literal* extinction—that all this was a result of a "necessary" process of "inevitable Progress," not to be made the subject of critical comment on pain of putting oneself outside the "inevitable movement" and criticising the patent "design" of "History." To such a conception of life and of history Scottish education has all along been committed and still addresses itself, following the state of consciousness and opinion desiderated by the Reformers and their descendants and fulfilling the implicit ends of their educational policy. Ninian Kennedy had foreseen it all long ago when, speaking of the Reformers' zeal for learning, he said— "The lear (education) that *ye* will gie them will be your doctrines (he might have said the imposition or instigation of your negating will) and the language of the English."

John Knox said: "What I have been to my country, albeit the present generation knows not, nevertheless future generations will testify," or words to that effect. He spoke more truly than he knew. From where we now stand it has become possible to see with unimpeded clarity that the triumph of the Reformation Party resulted first in the imposition everywhere of an anti-human ideology leading to the instigation throughout the community of a radical negating motivation, *and step by sure step thereafter to the final extinction of the Scottish nation, politically, culturally, linguistically, and in the end even biologically.*

It was inevitable. "Sin when it is finished bringeth forth Death." LOGICALLY AND ONTOLOGICALLY THE END OF NAY-SAY IS, SIMPLY, *NOTHING.*

One reflection remains. . . .

Although as we have seen no people or nation or "race" or particular age possesses a "Destiny" in the sense of a rôle apportioned to it in advance by any extra-historical or non-human Agent howsoever conceived and which it is bound to fulfil in spite of itself as part of some predetermined Design or Plan of History, nevertheless there is a sense in which every people or "race" or nation—as indeed every individual human being—can truly be said to possess a destiny. *That destiny is laid up for them in advance in the sum and character of their endowments, defined by their "given" potentialities, and fulfilled in proportion as those are realised in their actual life.*

Judged from this point of view one may say that the destiny of the Scots was of a distinction unique among peoples. The Albannaich, whoever they were, the collection of actual human persons assembled in the distant past in the geographical area we call Scotland, turned out to have been initially gifted with the element of sheer talent to a degree that had no parallel elsewhere. It has been frequently said, so that it is almost commonplace, that the Ancient Greeks, the Jews and the Scots have by the originality, force and substantive creativity of their native genius had a greater share in or more to do with the formation, character and achievements of the civilisation of the West than any other single people—and where the present West is concerned, and what is now rapidly becoming world civilisation, the premier distinction and substantive contribution belongs to the Scots. Not alone has there been the series of startling contributions resulting from the originality of individual genius, the repeated pulling down of a "new" thing out of the sky of infinite possibility—as for instance in our own immediate times, atomic science, penicillin, radar and television (associated with the names of Rutherford, Fleming, Watson Watt and Baird) have altered life for man in the world. But also, up till now every class and section of the community has continuously down the centuries given striking evidence of the presence in their midst of ability of great distinction, even of the greatest distinction short of such transcendent originality as we have above mentioned. (In my childhood the poorest and humblest element in the community might have been symbolised by the men who broke stones by the wayside. One addressed such men with respect—because they were men, in whose soul also the drama of human consciousness and destiny was being played in a unique setting, and because they were themselves very possibly intelligent men or gifted in some respect [if such a man, such a humble stonebreaker, were encountered in the Highlands he might well have been one of the greatest tellers of the traditional tales from the oral literature of Europe and therefore, had he known it, a man of international distinction in his own right]; but one spoke to such men with respect also because their brothers or other close relatives might well be—and probably were—distinguished professors, scientists or engineers of international repute, military officers of high rank, governors of imperial districts or provinces, or at the very least men successful to the point of eminence in commercial or industrial life.) Such a state of things did not obtain in any other national community in the world. In fact, if one may so put it, the Scottish community all along stank of ability.

Thanks to the direction given to activity by Reformationism, the view of life and the relative assessment of its values imposed by it, that ability has been inevitably exercised in limited areas and tended to be directed towards limited objectives, towards achievements in the sphere of the material element in life or of sheer "making one's way in the world"—such as science, engineering, the military art, medicine, commerce and manufacture. But had the men concerned been retained in the homeland as they would have been in an autonomously functioning national community (no other country exports its best), that is to say, had there never been that Reformation consequence a genocidal rate of emigration of the most gifted (and the concurrent and in the end equally genocidal immigration of non-Scottish elements of different human potential: of the present five million inhabitants of Scotland, two million must already be of non-Scottish or only part-Scottish origins), had the Reformation values and view of life never been—as they were universally—established but on the contrary a pro-human and not anti-human view presided over the life of the community, then—without necessary detriment to science, learning and the rest—*the whole of this unparalleled ability would have been applied over the whole range of the activities proper to man.* Further, had the process of Anglicisation never been introduced and imposed over the whole community, as it would never

203

have been but for the Reformation, the native traditions, which were of long descent and great vitality, instead of being systematically and unceremoniously ushered into the area of the unknown, would have been developed—and let it be remembered that while in the sphere of action a man of genius can in principle appear at any time, even among the most primitive peoples, where the intellectual and spritual side of man is concerned tradition is of the very life's-blood of all achievement, the base and necessary condition of all creative development no matter how original in the individual: and last, Anglicisation not having taken place, had the community retained, as it had in Gaelic, a language of immense strength and resources potentially equal to any other, and of unsurpassed mellifluence—had all those conditions been fulfilled (in other words, had the community not taken with the Reformation a vertiginous plunge into anti-culture) then the community of Albannaich instead of falling to the condition of "the greatest cultural desert in Europe," would *necessarily* have developed into a veritable oasis of unexcelled fertility and of vast extent in the area of the human spirit.

IN OTHER WORDS, WHAT THE REFORMATION DID WAS TO SNUFF OUT WHAT MUST OTHERWISE HAVE DEVELOPED INTO THE MOST BRILLIANT NATIONAL CULTURE IN HISTORY.